MW00399733

THE GOSPEL TRUTH
About MONEY
MANAGEMENT

THE GOSPEL TRUTH *About* MONEY MANAGEMENT
Making Every Dollar Count

Judy Woodward Bates

New Hope Publishers
Birmingham, Alabama

New Hope Publishers
P. O. Box 12065
Birmingham, AL 35202-2065
www.newhopepubl.com

© 2003 by Judy Woodward Bates
All rights reserved. First printing 2003
Printed in the United States of America

Bargainomics® is a registered trademark of Judy Woodward Bates.

No part of this publication may be reproduced, stored in a retrieval system, or transmitted in any form or by any means—electronic, mechanical, photocopying, recording, or otherwise—without the prior written permission of the publisher.

Library of Congress Cataloging-in-Publication Data
Bates, Judy Woodward, 1952-
   The Gospel truth about money management: making every dollar count / by Judy Woodward Bates.
   p. cm.
   ISBN 1-56309-724-9
1. Finance, Personal-Religious aspects-Christianity. I. Title.
   HG179 .B343 2003
   332.024—dc21
                          2002012366

All Scripture quotations, unless otherwise indicated, are taken from the NEW AMERICAN STANDARD BIBLE®, Copyright © 1960, 1962, 1963, 1968, 1971, 1972, 1973, 1975, 1977, 1995 by The Lockman Foundation. Used by permission.

Scripture quotations marked (NIV) are taken from the HOLY BIBLE, NEW INTERNATIONAL VERSION®. NIV®. Copyright©1973, 1978, 1984 by International Bible Society. Used by permission of Zondervan. All rights reserved.

Scripture quotations marked (AMP) are taken from the Amplified Bible, Copyright © 1954, 1958, 1962, 1964, 1965, 1987 by The Lockman Foundation. Used by permission.

Scripture quotations marked (TLB) are taken from *The Living Bible*, Copyright© 1971. Used by permission of Tyndale House Publishers, Inc., Wheaton, IL. All rights reserved.

Scripture quotations marked (ASV) are taken from The Holy Bible, American Standard Version.

Scripture quotations marked (KJV) are taken from The Holy Bible, King James Version.

Cover design by Righteous Planet
Back cover photo by Paula McCarty
Interior illustrations by Millie Caffee and Bruce Watford

ISBN: 1-56309-724-9

N024123 • 0103 • 10M1

Dedication

First and foremost, I dedicate this book to my Lord Jesus Christ, without whom I can do nothing.

Secondly, to the greatest encourager and lifemate I could ever ask for, my husband and friend Larry Bates.

To the world's utmost webmaster and computer guru Tim Vines, and to his wife Lisa, without whom my hair would always be a mess.

And to one remarkable cousin, friend, artist, and traveling companion, Millie Caffee.

Last but not remotely least, my Long Island "Yankee" buddy, Alice Ross, deserves a huge thanks for coming up with the perfect title for this book.

I love you all very, very much.

Table of Contents

Meet the
Bargainomics Lady

"She is energetic, a hard worker, and watches for bargains."

—Proverbs 31:17–18

"Wery glad to see you, indeed, and hope our acquaintance may be a long 'un . . ."

—Sam Weller,
in Charles Dickens' *The Pickwick Papers*

et me introduce myself! My real name is Judy Woodward Bates, but to many people I'm known as the Bargainomics® Lady. How did I get this title? The Lord has given me a ministry of helping people learn the wisest possible use of time, money, and resources for the glory of God. Whether we have a lot of money or just a little, God wants us to handle it wisely so that we aren't slaves to money and so that we can glorify Him in our lives! That's what Bargainomics® is all about.

I've spent my adult life collecting ways to stretch pennies to the max while living joyfully and well. Sometimes I've done it out of necessity during lean times for my family, but mostly I do this because I believe my money is really God's money. I want to be a wise steward and hear Him say, "Well, done, thou good and faithful servant."

The whole Bargainomics® story began when my husband was laid off from his job and was unemployed for two years. During those two blessed educational years, we both learned many valuable lessons about the value of a dollar. We learned that no honest job was beneath our dignity. We mowed lawns, cleaned houses, and did whatever it took to keep our household stable. Many of the tips and ideas that came to be Bargainomics® were discovered during that time. It was then that I discovered the treasure troves of yard sales, thrift stores, and consignment shops. Most of all, it was then that I learned how much I could trust the real treasure, the ever-faithful Lord Jesus Christ.

I became the Bargainomics® Lady much later, when my dear friend Cheryl Tolar, knowing my penchant for money-saving ideas, asked me to speak to the ladies of her church. A local television station showed up and taped part of the presentation.

The next thing I knew, I was getting invitations to be on talk shows and news programs. A Christian radio station gave me my own half-hour radio show on the Christian principles of money management. A television station gave me a regular spot on its noonday news show. I discovered that there was a great need out there for the discipline of Christian money management. Women were hungry for this, not just for the financial benefits but also for the spiritual benefits! This was an everyday, ongoing way for us to practice God's will for our lives in small and large ways.

As invitations to speak to churches and civic groups kept coming, I realized I needed a name for this ministry. I was attending seminary classes at that time, as part of the Women's Ministry program of New Orleans Baptist Theological Seminary. During a break between classes, my brilliant fellow seminarians and I came up with the word Bargainomics®.

What could have been more appropriate! One of the passages I loved to use when I was speaking is from Proverbs 31—the verses about the virtuous woman. In the *Living Bible* paraphrase, verses 17 and 18 read:

"She is energetic, a hard worker, and watches for bargains."

For the first time, the virtuous woman and I had a few things in common! Bargainomics®. The word was custom-made to describe this ministry.

A Lifelong Discipline

Throughout my life, God provided me with people who gave me a sense of the value of time, of money, of love and relationship, the value of God's creation. The more I understand my life, the more I realize everything good really does come from God. Every last little thing. That's why I want to help others make the most of what God has given them, to squeeze the most joy and nourishment that they can from life. Not to waste a drop.

My parents set the example for me. My father was a brick mason. My mother, like most moms in those days, stayed home with me and my sister Diane. I grew up in Graysville, Alabama, a small town near Birmingham. Our little city's society was more blue-collar than blueblood—most fathers who weren't steelworkers were coal miners.

I was the youngest of 32 grandchildren. Big Mama Woodward was the daughter of a circuit-riding Methodist preacher. Papa was a carpenter. After years with one company he was laid off, pensionless and penniless. He set up shop in the big garage behind his house on the Old Bankhead Highway and turned out wooden wonders for grandchildren, paying customers, and those who couldn't pay.

When we grandchildren visited them, just before bedtime Papa and Big Mama would call us into the living room, and Papa would read his Bible aloud. Afterwards they would slip down onto their knees and lead us in the sweetest of prayers—for our family, our country, our world.

My family was active at a small Methodist church. When I was ten, I was stunned and moved to see my father come forward to receive Jesus Christ as Lord and Savior. My father! The faithful churchgoer, the choir member, was confessing his need to be saved! My heart was pounding as I thought, "That's what I need, too," and my little feet followed my daddy's down the aisle.

Meet Prince Charming

By the time I entered high school, both Big Mama and Papa had gone to be with the Lord, and we had moved into their house. One day as I was wandering the halls at school, I glimpsed a handsome, dark-haired, brown-eyed guy, wearing a purple number 55 football jersey and hobbling along on crutches. I soon discovered that the injured athlete/Prince Charming was a senior and would be graduating in a few short weeks. Cruelest of jokes! I wrote us off as two ships in the night.

That summer, my cousin Ginger picked me up in her

1967 Camaro convertible and whisked me away to Teen Valley, a new dance club for teenagers. There on the dance floor was the form of the dark-haired hunk from Minor High School—without his crutches. Next thing I knew, Ginger had pulled Larry over to meet me.

"Want to dance?" he smiled, reaching for my hand.

After a while Larry asked if he could drive me home. Walking me to the door, he asked for a real, live date, and thus began my journey to becoming Mrs. Larry W. Bates on February 27, 1970. We were married in a lovely little church wedding only a few months before I finished high school at age 17. Larry was 20 and was attending a local junior college while working for US Steel, where my dad and granddad had worked.

Although Larry and I were both professing Christians and we attended pretty much all the services at our church, we did not tithe and were not students of the Bible; and we certainly had no serious shared or separate quiet times. Our concept of faith was immature at best. After our son Mickey was born in 1973, we began to think far more seriously about our "church life."

Something Missing

Growth for Larry came day by day, seemingly moment by moment. We began tithing and taking on responsibilities within the church. Larry was eventually ordained as a deacon. We'd both begun teaching classes at church. We had built a new home, had wonderful neighbors, our family was happy and healthy, and Larry's income allowed us to live comfortably. Life was good. I should have been the happiest person on earth, but in truth, I felt unfulfilled. I worked hard at seeming to have it all together, but deep inside I needed something else to make my life complete.

Watching Larry become more and more at peace, more and more grounded in his faith, I became certain that he had something I didn't. I was missing out and had no idea why. The void in my life was tangible, the emptiness was constant. What, what, what was wrong with me?

One night while my husband and son were fast asleep, I went into the living room and began to pray, asking God to show me what was wrong, what was needed to rid me of the terrible hollowness I felt inside. There were no bells, no lights, no bolts of thunder, and yet the Holy Spirit so permeated that room that I knew beyond any shadow of doubt that I was in God's presence. Although there was no audible voice, I clearly heard Him speak to my heart.

He lovingly showed me that while I had taken the right steps, I'd taken them all with my head and not my heart. Never had I fully surrendered to the Lordship and leading of Jesus Christ. *He* was what I was missing. The void in my life was God-shaped. He alone could fill that space.

Then and there I truly surrendered all—my life, my hopes, my everything. The moment I did, the Holy Spirit came into my life in a new way, filling that aching, gaping hole with a presence so real that I knew that I knew that I knew my life had been changed. I was not and never would be the same.

Ever merciful, the Lord allowed me the next few years to mature in Him before, in 1982, US Steel virtually shut its doors and our safe, secure income was no longer there! We quickly learned that there remained one constant Who was never going to leave us or forsake us (Hebrews 13:5).

After the Layoff

From day one, Larry and I had agreed that I was to manage our money. He trusted me implicitly, and I was determined to be worthy of his confidence. Having married so young, I was also determined not to turn to our parents for financial assistance. But with the layoff, my skills were tested and honed. I worked part-time and temporary jobs to bring in money while still being home for our son Mickey. I tried my hand at real estate, remodeling houses, substitute teaching, and a host of other things.

I had always loved to write but hadn't done much since high school. A few years after Larry went back to work at US Steel, I went to work at UAB Hospital (University of Alabama at Birmingham). The pharmacy department newsletter was soon (and divinely) added to my responsibilities. During those years I began to write my own lessons for the classes I taught at church. The response encouraged me, so I tried a bit of freelancing and was thrilled to discover that someone was actually willing to pay me!

Through the influence of friends such as Sammie Barstow, David and Joanne Sloan, Cheryl Wray, and Dr. Mike Fink, I attended writing conferences and developed my writing skills, and completed the Women's Ministry Certificate Program under Dr. Rhonda Kelley at New Orleans Baptist Theological Seminary.

And Now?

Aside from a car payment (which I intend to be short-lived) and the usual monthly expenses for utilities, insurance, and so on, Larry and I have no debts. We practice tithing—giving a tenth of our income to the church—and are often able to give above and beyond our tithe.

We find that God blesses that obedience in so many ways we can't count them! We find peace and freedom in God's way of living. We find that God's "enough" is richer and more satisfying than what the world says is "enough." We find that variety and fun and joy in life don't have to come with a huge price tag.

God wants you to experience this abundant life, too. It's available, and it's free! Read on, and you may find that Bargainomics® is your path to learning the wisest possible use of time, money, and resources for the glory of God.

Chapter 1

Explaining Bargainomics

"That ye may do that which is honorable.
. . . For this cause I write these things."
                    —2 Corinthians 13:7, 10 ASV

"This, books can do—nor this alone: they give
New views to life, and teach us how to live;
They soothe the grieved, the stubborn they chastise;
Fools they admonish, and confirm the wise.
Their aid they yield to all."
            —George Crabbe, *The Library*, **1754–1832**

Just What Is Bargainomics?

Simply put,

Bargainomics® *is the wisest possible use of time, money, and resources for the glory of God.*

When we recognize the Lord Jesus Christ as the true owner of all we have and are, this realization should give us a whole new perspective on how we spend our lives.

We are told in 1 Corinthians 6:19b-20a (NIV): "You are not your own; you were bought at a price." If you have experienced new birth in Christ Jesus, then this verse applies to you. And once you understand that your entire being belongs to the Lord, then it is easier to catch hold of the fact that you are accountable to Him for every aspect of your life!

Consider Jesus' parable of the shrewd manager, found in Luke 16. He begins by saying: "There was a rich man whose manager was accused of wasting his possessions" (Luke 16:1 NIV). The rich man had given this manager the job of watching over his belongings, and that manager had not been responsible, had not acted in his master's best interest.

Jesus concluded by telling His listeners: "So if you have not been trustworthy in handling worldly wealth, who will trust you with true riches?" (Luke 16:11 NIV) As Lord of all, He expects us to be the best possible managers of everything with which He entrusts us—and that includes every single part of our lives, including time and money.

Does this mean we are to cut back to bread and water and start cruising on trash day for cast-off clothing? No. What it does mean is that we should *prayerfully* use our resources. In 1 Corinthians 10:1 (AMP) Paul told the believers: "For I do not want you to be ignorant, brethren."

When we are irresponsible with time and money, we are squandering the precious gifts of God. Can we do this and merely plead ignorance? Again, no, and you can be sure I can back that up with Scripture, too.

First Corinthians 1:30 (NIV) declares of believers: "You are in Christ Jesus, who has become for us wisdom from God—that is, our righteousness, holiness and redemption." Did you catch that? *"For us."* No wonder Paul went on to say we shouldn't be ignorant!

Don't let anyone tell you or make you feel that you aren't smart—everything you and I need to know in order to be good managers is within us through the indwelling of the Holy Spirit. He is the One whom Jesus declared would "guide you into all the truth" (John 16:13).

Truth is, we have a Heavenly Father who loves to bless His children. In Matthew 7:11 Jesus taught the people: "If you . . . know how to give good gifts to your children, how much more will your Father who is in heaven give what is good to those who ask Him!" The "name-it-and-claim-its" would have us to believe that this verse gives us the right to demand of God, to expect Him to deliver whatever we have put on our want lists. But let's move over to Luke 11:13 and perhaps get a better understanding of what Jesus is telling us in this passage: "If you . . . know how to give good gifts to your children, how much more will your heavenly Father give the Holy Spirit to those who ask Him?" What greater gift is there than the Holy Spirit?

This brings up another question: How much of the Holy Spirit do we get when we are saved? Ephesians 1:13 gives us that answer: "And you also were included in Christ when you heard the word of truth, the gospel of your salvation. Having believed, you were marked in him with a seal, the promised Holy Spirit" (NIV).

Look at the progression in that verse. First, the person *heard* the word. Next, he *believed*. And upon that person's belief, he was *marked with a seal*—that is, permanently stamped as belonging to Christ. How? By the Holy Spirit, coming to live inside that new believer's heart.

How do we know this is permanent? The very next verse answers that one: "who [the Holy Spirit] is a deposit guaranteeing our inheritance" (Ephesians 1:14 NIV). Ain't no *ifs* or *maybes* about it, y'all. The third person of the Holy Trinity, God Himself, *guarantees* that He "will never desert you, nor . . . forsake you" (Hebrews 13:5).

Many of the principles, tips, and ideas that are incorporated into this book can be applied by virtually anyone,

Christian or not. But my heart is speaking to you from a relationship with Jesus Christ, one that has made bargain-hunting and time-saving a joyful lifestyle for me. Finding the best buys has become an exciting adventure. Learning a way to shave a few minutes off a work project puts a smile on my face—and extra minutes in my day!

"Lord, multiply my time!" I often pray. And He who is infinitely faithful does just that. I pray before I shop. Literally. Even to find the discounted meats and produce in the supermarket. Even to spot the very best markdown in the retail store.

How Bargainomics Helped Me

Bargainomics® has helped me to buy a home far below market value and to live in and restore that home mort-gage-free. I've found that properties, vehicles, jewelry, furniture, clothing, gifts, groceries, vacations, virtually anything can be bought for far less than the average con-sumer expects to pay.

To save time, I've discovered ways to accomplish more in one day than I used to think was even possible. And just as importantly, I've learned to get these things done without feeling frantic, without feeling as though I'm carrying the weight of the world on my shoulders.

The more the Lord teaches me about Bargainomics®, the more pumped I get about sharing this information with others. But be warned! The Bargainomics® lifestyle is both contagious and addictive. I hope you're ready for a debt-free, better organized life, 'cause if you keep on reading and apply what you find, those results will pretty much be inevitable.

Explaining Bargainomics   17

Chapter 2

On Credit

"The borrower is servant to the lender."
—**Proverbs 22:7 KJV**

*"You're old enough that your wants
won't hurt you."*
—**William Ellis Woodward (my daddy)**

I'm sure my daddy wasn't the first person to admonish anyone by saying "Your wants won't hurt you," but he was the first person to teach me that I actually need to *have* money in order to spend it. Now that might not seem like much of a revelation, but when you take a look at these statistics* on credit card debt, your eyes will begin to open, if not pop right out of their sockets:

1. American adults own somewhere in the neighborhood of 1.6 *billion* credit and charge cards, many of which are maxed out.
2. The typical American family lays claim to 6 cards, each of which indebts them for over $4,000. Do the math—we're talking $24,000!!!!
(*Source: www.thedebttrap.com)

So what's the best advice I can give you about finding a good credit card?

Don't do it!

See, I told you this book was simple. Never, never, never, never, never use credit to make any purchase other than your home or car. Okay, that may be a slight exaggeration, but if you're struggling with credit debt, it's the new mentality you need to absorb.

Granted, you may be one of those rare individuals

who can actually use a credit card responsibly and pay the full balance each month. If you are, congratulations! You are a rare bird indeed. (And please keep reading. This book addresses all people within all incomes, regardless of their current spending habits.)

But for most folks, such is not the case. By and large, *people use credit cards to buy what they don't have the money to pay for*—and the resulting debt wreaks havoc on their self-esteem, relationships, and every aspect of their lives.

If you're one of those caught in credit card chaos, does this mean you're up the creek without the proverbial paddle? No! It simply means that you are now in a position to trust God like you never have before. But what does trusting God have to do with credit spending, you ask?

One of the Old Testament names of God is *Jehovah Jireh*, which means, "God provides." In Philippians 4:19 the apostle Paul reminds us: "And my God will supply all your needs according to His riches in glory in Christ Jesus." If the Lord Jesus Christ is your God, He stands ready and willing to meet your needs today.

Note that Philippians 4:19 addresses *needs*, not wants. My daddy's advice bears repeating: "You're old enough that your wants won't hurt you." We who live in this society of immediate gratification need to clearly differentiate between our *needs* and our *wants*. You might *want* a 30-room mansion in Beverly Hills, but what you *need* is simply a roof over your head. You may want two weeks at the Hilton when your checkbook points to a weekend at Motel 6. I realize that's a bit of oversimplification, but you get the idea.

So what do you do? You look at that checkbook and you look at that shimmering rectangle of plastic. Decisions, decisions. You'll either choose to work with what you have or you will opt for the plastic, which translates to living beyond your means.

Stop right now and find one of your credit cards. Put it in your hand and take a good look at it. It's plastic, right? Now, keep one hand on the credit card and absorb this. What does the word plastic mean? Some of the synonyms are *artificial*, *fake*, *synthetic*, *false*. Take a good look at that card and then go through this list of definitions aloud. Look that card square in the face and call it what it is: Artificial! Fake! Synthetic! False!

Horror of horrors, it's all true, isn't it? That credit card is *artificial* wealth, a *fake* asset, *synthetic* success, and a *false* status symbol.

A Tale of Whoa

To help us get a grip on the truth of credit's falsehood, let's look at a scenario. You're single and, of course, stunningly attractive. At a recent social function you met Prince Charmingest (superior to merely Charming) and he asked you for a date. (If you're a guy, just switch your scenario to stunningly handsome and Princess Charmingest.) You checked your daybook and casually agreed to see him.

On the appointed evening PC (as Prince Charmingest is called by his friends) arrives in a stretch limo and whisks you away to a performance of the Alpenhorn Symphony, followed by dinner at the finest French restaurant in town, Chateau de Wow. Dessert, he insists, will be served on the veranda of his home.

The driver takes you to the gates of an imposing mansion, presses a code into the keypad, and the gates swing open. You're whisked up a winding, brick-paved drive and deposited in front of a three-story antebellum mega-mansion where PC casually unlocks the door and leads the way through several exquisitely decorated rooms and out onto a wide sitting area overlooking a pool, courtyard, and gardens.

Explaining that the staff has been given the evening off, PC serves up fresh, hot espresso and a crème brulee to die for. You chat, you drink in the perfect starry night, and, after gentle but meaningful lip-to-lip contact, he has his driver return you to your home. That night you fall asleep wondering if this could be the beginning of a truly beautiful friendship.

Things are progressing wonderfully between you and the Prince, although you find it strange that all your dates have been on Thursday evenings. One Saturday, on a whim, you decide to pack a picnic lunch and bundle PC off for a lakeside adventure.

Pulling up to the gates of Camelot (the name you felt was appropriate for PC's dwelling), you press the intercom button, smiling and checking yourself in your visor mirror. A bored voice queries, "State your name and business, please."

"I'm Stunningly Attractive," you announce, "and I'm here to see PC."

The voice takes on a tone of undisguised contempt. "The employees are not allowed to receive visitors through the main gate," you are told. "You'll need to drive around to the service entrance in the rear."

"Excuse me," you sputter, thoroughly confused, "I'm here to see the owner, Prince Charmingest himself. Just give him my name. He knows who I am," you retort with a smirk. *There*, you think. *That'll set the record straight.*

But not so. "Ms. Attractive," the voice now speaks through a full set of clenched teeth, "Prince Charmingest is the chauffeur, not the owner, and I suggest you contact him on a Thursday, which is his regularly scheduled day off."

You back away from the gate and head for the lakeside alone. Luckily, you've packed quite a hamper, and food has always been a great comfort to you, even when your heart's broken. A loaf of french bread, a fried chicken, and a quart of potato salad later, you manage to drive yourself home. (I can only envision the way I'd deal with it, okay?)

You see, Stunningly Attractive discovered that her prince was a phony. He didn't own the limo. He didn't own the house. If Charles the butler hadn't agreed to open up the house and pose as the driver, the guy would never have been able to pull off such a scam. Sad but true, everything about PC was a crock—a pretense, subterfuge, *artificial*, *fake*, *synthetic*, *false*. Are we starting to get the picture here?

Living on credit isn't living—it's fantasy. And if there's one thing a believer in Jesus Christ ought to be, it's for real. Proverbs 13:7 says it like this: "There is one who pretends to be rich, but has nothing." If you are looking for your satisfaction in anything other than your relationship with the Lord Jesus Christ, it's time to re-focus your priorities.

Who's the Boss?

Okay, here's the next step, and it gets even tougher. (Hey, love has to be tough. I love you enough to want you to get real with yourself.) Still got that credit card in your hand? Head for the nearest mirror and hold that thing up right beside your face and look at the two of you together. If you are living on credit, every attribute of that credit card also applies to you.

Having said that, get ready to absorb this: *You cannot depend on God and credit when it comes to the area of finance.* I've tried to cover the disclaimers already, like transportation and housing, but let me reiterate and elaborate just a bit right here.

Owing for a **needed** home and/or vehicle is perfectly reasonable. On the other hand, if your paychecks disappear paying other types of credit debt (especially unsecured purchases) then you, my friend, have a problem, and the solution, according to both me and Barney Fife, is to "Nip it in the bud!"

Which brings us back to the tale of Stunningly Attractive and Prince Charmingest. PC was pretending to own things that were not his. We, when we use credit to have or do things we can't otherwise afford, are doing the very same thing. So doing, we are expressing our dissatisfaction with where and who we are in this life. And the critical thing to realize is that this should not be the issue! What *is* important is **whose** we are.

Paul makes that astounding announcement in 1 Corinthians 6:19b-20a (NIV): "You are not your own; you were bought at a price." If you have ever accepted Jesus Christ as your Lord and Savior, you belong to Him—"you are not your own." He paid the ransom for your life through His own substitutionary death—"you were bought at a price."

Because of this unbreakable relationship, you are obligated to your Savior. You should not be obligated to credit debt. Why do I say this? The Amplified Bible puts it this way: "No one can serve two masters; for either he will hate the one and love the other, or he will stand by and be devoted to the one and despise and be against the other. You cannot serve God and mammon [that is, deceitful riches, money, possessions, or what is trusted in]" (Matthew 6:24).

And remember, this is Jesus speaking in this verse. If you look back at the opening page of this chapter, you'll see Proverbs 22:7 (KJV): "The borrower is servant to the lender." Credit debt is exactly what the term *credit* implies. It is a loan that you are required to repay—with interest.

Let's Take Our Medicine

This may be a hard pill to swallow, but bear in mind: *When we focus on the cure and not the treatment, it becomes much easier to take the medicine.* Perhaps you're already in trouble financially—you're behind on your payments; you dread checking the mail or answering the telephone. Please don't despair. There is help available.

Let me say here that I realize a small percentage of you who are reading this book got into debt during a time that was pretty much out of your control: a spouse left or passed away; a catastrophic illness drained your finances. Any number of circumstances could have quickly and drastically altered your financial situation.

Whatever caused your indebtedness, it's important to look at the whole picture, the starting point of which may really surprise you. I checked the word *debt* in a diction-ary. Care to guess what I came up with? *Sin*; *tresspass*; *obligation*. And the first synonym listed? *Evil.* No, I didn't make that up—it's true. Check it out for yourself.

Today we have all these fluffy phrases like "alterna-tive lifestyle" and "product of society" we use to couch what is actually plain ol' ugly sin. Is it any wonder we give another name to the sin of irresponsible money manage-ment?

Irresponsible debt and sin are interchangeable. If you have been an irresponsible money manager, stop right now, repent (which means turn in the opposite direction), and make a commitment to the Lord and to yourself to begin anew as a wise manager of His blessings. Ask Him to guide you as you walk on the road of recovery. And note it's a road and not a hallway. You didn't get in debt overnight, and neither will you get out quickly.

Without Credit, How Do I Build Up a Good Credit Profile?

Always keep receipts for major purchases. Being ready to show your ability to make major purchases in cash is pret-ty impressive, not just to me and your friends, but to cred-it gurus as well. When applying for a car loan or home mortgage, be prepared to present copies (not the originals) of your major purchase cash receipts. Having a bunch of credit purchases to your record is not necessary.

The Old Gas Card Ploy

"Ah but," you say, "I need my gas card to keep up with my gas purchases." No you don't. Ask for receipts and pay cash. Have you noticed that, like other cards, gas cards give you an opportunity to forestall full payment at the end of the month? Not only does the statement show the balance owed on the card, it also shows the "minimum amount due." By paying the minimum on your card, you can owe for last year's gas this time next year! And that is *not* intelligent financial management.

Don't let these or any other card companies con you with the great rebates. Most offer a maximum 3% rebate on your purchases. At that rate, if you use a credit card to buy $1,000 worth of gas over the next year, you'll have received a whopping 30 bucks in free gasoline over that same period. This sounds great until you realize that, whoops!—there you are unable to pay your monthly balance in full. The 30 big ones go out the window along with a whole lot more you have to pay in interest.

And haven't you noticed that most gas cards have become major credit cards as well? For example, let's create the Mistercard. Credit limits of $5,000 or more are common for these. By offering 3% rebates on gas and 1% on all other purchases, a combined expenditure of $3,000 ($1,000 on gas and $2,000 on other) would net the indebted person a $50 credit. When you look at the interest you are paying, since, like most people, you manage to slip into that "I-can't-pay-the-full-balance-each-month" mode, you are *losing* money in the long run.

The Dreaded Department Store Card

Zero percent interest? Can this be? Sure, some stores offer this option. One store I know offers six months' free interest. If you buy $300 in merchandise, your payment is $50 per month for six months. But the question again is, ***Why buy it if you can't afford to pay cash?*** The gimmick here again is that you are offered an interest-free plan and an "optional payment plan" on the same statement. It's soooo easy to choose that much lower optional payment. Lower for the present moment, yes; but you will also be paying interest out the wazoo (I'll leave this location to your imagination) and making payments for a long time.

What about these offers for "no payment until 2025"? Read the fine print, honey. Your interest accrues—begins adding up—from the moment you sign your name on the dotted line. This is true even if the line is not dotted!

Yes, but there are also those "no payment, no interest until . . ." credit offers. 'Splain that one, you say. Check around. Price the same item elsewhere and you'll find, in most cases, it costs far less at other places. These "no interest" businesses are simply shrewd enough to add plenty of extra profit to the purchase price. What *looks* like interest-free buying is really costing you big-time.

But How Can I Order By Phone?

Any reputable business that offers you the chance to phone in an order will also allow you to mail them a personal check, cashier's check, or money order. See how simple it is? Call the number, ask for the mailing address, sit down right then, and write out your order and mail it!

Just like places where you can actually go and see and touch the merchandise, these places want your business. They will be happy to figure your shipping charges and other possible expenses and tell you exactly how much you'll need to send with your order. (Another idea is the debit card. Keep reading—you're almost there.)

I know, I can hear you whining right now, saying, "But mailing will take too long." If this is an order for some life-saving drug you need, I suggest you head down to your local pharmacy and pick it up. Otherwise, don't use time as an excuse to indebt yourself—the time you spend working overtime or at a second job to pay for these things can be better spent elsewhere, right? Besides, if you're really desperate, you can always ask about paying for express delivery. Many places offer overnight and three-day delivery if you're willing to pay extra.

What About Online Shopping?

Same thing. Many companies will allow you to go ahead and place your order, which will then be held for processing until your payment is received. Others may not offer this option, but you can still choose your merchandise online, copy or print out the order form, and then mail your payment and order.

If you must use a credit card to order something online, keep up with what you are spending, including shipping, handling, and any other charges. Be sure you have the cash on hand to pay for the item and know the final total before you commit to the order. As soon as the statement arrives, pay in full.

But I *Need* a Major Credit Card

Not unless you can be responsible with it. The only reason you truly need a major credit card is to enable you to do things like hold hotel reservations, rent cars, pay for airline tickets, etc., and a debit card (see below) can do the very same thing for you. If you can't discipline yourself to maintain a zero balance, then get rid of the card. The good old mail-'em-a-check method will take care of anything your credit card could have done for you. This may be surprising, but I have found few businesses that have a problem accepting cash, which makes a debit card, when used intelligently, an even handier solution.

Debit Cards

Your bank probably offers a debit card, complete with the name of a major card company. This is simply a card that allows you to make purchases exactly as you would with a credit card, except that the amount for each purchase is deducted directly from your checking account. In other words, it may look like plastic, but it's real honest-to-goodness cold hard cash. Anything you can do with a credit card, you can do with a debit card; the beautiful part is that, with any transaction, *you must have the cash to back up your purchase.*

As with an ATM (automatic teller machine) card, be careful to write down each purchase and keep your receipts to ensure that the correct amounts are deducted from your checking account. I cannot stress this strongly enough—I've heard far too many tales of woe from those who failed to keep good records of debit card spending and suffered serious consequences.

Also, be sure you know exactly what this card will cost you. Your bank or credit union may charge a small annual fee for allowing you to carry the card; and some businesses may charge a fee per transaction as well.

Don't pay anything unnecessarily. Find a bank that offers their cards fee-free. Ask about extra fees whenever presenting your card in unfamiliar places, and steer clear of debit card use in "fee" spots.

Chapter Summary and Closing Thoughts

1. You don't *need* a credit card. You may want one, but needing and wanting are two different things.

Anything a credit card can do for you, cash, a personal or cashier's check, or a money order can also do.

2. Everybody likes cash. Use it wisely, but use it. Credit is not necessary, even to receive a good credit rating. And remember, a debit card is cash. Don't use it unless you can afford to turn loose the amount of real live cash money your purchase requires.

3. Speaking of cash, use it, literally. Allot a reasonable amount to carry around with you and make your purchases in cash whenever possible. There's something about plunking down those genuine greenbacks that makes a person think twice before they're willing to turn them loose. Discipline yourself to leave that checkbook at home and stop spending when the cash in your wallet is gone.

4. Trust the Lord. Your Heavenly Father loves you and cares about every aspect of your life, including finances. Pray before and as you spend money. Ask for His guidance in making wise choices. You'll be amazed at the difference in how far those dollars will stretch.

Chapter 3

Shopping

"And upon finding one pearl of great value, he went and sold all that he had and bought it."
—Matthew 13:46

"A bargain isn't a bargain unless you need it."
—William Ellis Woodward
(my daddy's advice again)

Born to Shop?

Like the bumper sticker says, some women seem to be truly "born to shop." For those of you who love nothing better than a day at the mall, just remember that you are treading in Temptation Alley. If you can go, look around, have lunch or dinner, and return home without having done needless damage to your wallet or, horror of horrors, used a credit card to finance your outing, then have at it.

But if you can't resist that spending urge, stay away. Don't use lunch plans, meeting friends, or boredom as excuses to go out and unwisely spend money.

For some of us, shopping is such fun, isn't it? For others, it's a horrible drudgery to be done only when absolutely necessary. Whichever category most closely describes you, this chapter can transform you into a brilliant Bargainomics® shopper. Bear in mind, too, that these tips apply to shopping in general and not just to clothing shopping.

This brings us back to what my daddy always says about spending money:

A bargain isn't a bargain unless you need it.

If you have no reason to be buying, then don't. Perhaps the best way to change your shopping habits is to call them what they are: *spending* habits. Next time you think of going out to buy, say to yourself, "I'm going *spending*," rather than "I'm going shopping." This little discipline will help you realize and rectify your shopping shortfalls.

If you're one of those who love to shop or if you're just someone who wants to learn to get the very most out of your shopping experience, I need to introduce to you the Occasions List.

The Occasions List

At the beginning of each year (do this right now if you want to go ahead and get started), I take a sheet of paper and, down the left side, I list the names of every person that I plan to buy a gift for all year. I also list bridal teas, baby teas, and graduations so that I can note extra gifts I pick up to cover those unexpected invitations—as you probably know from experience, there seem to be some people who go through the church directory and send out invitations to the whole congregation!

Out beside each name I list the person's birthday and any other significant dates, favorite colors, hobbies, sizes—any pertinent info I want to make note of. I fold the paper and stick it in my wallet. Then throughout the year, each time I shop, I'm on the lookout for items to fill my occasions list. As I make a purchase, I note it in the appropriate spot.

For example, let's say I'm out shopping in January and I find a super buy on a great-looking purple sweatshirt. I whip out my list and see that the size is just right for

Uncle Herman and, lo and behold, purple is his favorite color. I buy it and jot "C-purple s/shirt" beside Uncle Herman's name ("C" denoting that this gift is for Christmas).

Using an occasions list year round means usually having gifts ready well in advance of every occasion. No rushing out at the last minute to pay premium dollars for a not-so-premium gift. Best of all, way before Christmastime arrives, you'll have finished your shopping and, since the expense was spread throughout the year, your wallet won't be empty and you won't be out there fighting the holiday shopping mob.

Of course, if you're buying gifts all year round, you need a place to store that stuff, don't you? Designate a specific area as your gift closet or shelf, whatever amount of room you can spare or think you'll need.

Don't Be Afraid to Ask

As you shop, always ask for boxes. Most retail stores give them, and if you'll ask, you might be very surprised at what other freebies are available. One retailer I frequent gives the box, wrapping paper, tissue paper, ribbon, bow, and gift card! And they offer the option of doing your wrapping free of charge or letting you take all these goodies with you.

They don't advertise this fact. How'd I find out? I asked.

Don't be afraid to ask. The worst thing they can tell you is "No." This is a phrase you're going to hear from me over and over.

Ask them: Do you give boxes? What else is available? Paper? Ribbon? Bow? Gift card? No one is going to throw you out of the store for inquiring. Too, if making a purchase makes you eligible to receive these things, it's irrelevant who the merchandise was purchased for. Request these perks even when you're buying items for your own use.

In some stores, a limited amount of boxes and related supplies are available at each sales counter. Other stores keep all such stock in the gift-wrap area. If the latter is the case, complete all your shopping and make one visit to gift-wrap.

Find out if there's a charge for gift-wrapping. Some stores offer one free gift-wrap and more elaborate wrapping for a fee. If you allow the store to wrap your gift, make certain your selection is free of charge.

I learned this lesson when I had a wedding gift wrapped several years ago. I inquired and was told that the store did offer a free gift-wrap. As the lady began pulling out paper for my package, I pointed to a different roll and asked if she could use that pattern instead. She nodded, wrapped my gift, and promptly charged me several dollars. When I protested, she informed me that the fee was imposed any time their "regular" paper wasn't used.

Gift Closet

Set apart an area of your home for storing and organizing your gifts and gift-wrap. A closet or even just a shelf will do nicely. How will you fit in a year's worth of gifts? Simple. As you bring home new items, go ahead and box them up. Use a pencil to write the intended recipient's name on the bottom of the box. The boxes will stack neatly and take up very little space. Also, half the battle's over when it's time to do all that wrapping.

When to Shop

Day of the week. Are some days better times to shop than others? Unquestionably, yes. Mondays are often great days to catch "unadvertised" specials, since Mondays are typically slow days in most stores. Also, anytime you know of an upcoming sale, you'll often wind up with first dibs on the bargains if you'll go a day or two before the official sale begins. Items are often marked down early.

Seasons for shopping. Let me begin by saying that virtually everything is seasonal. As seasons change, so does the merchandise. Stock for jewelry, shoes, even cosmetics, furniture, and housewares undergo plenty of changes.

Naturally, after-Christmas sales can be terrific, but since at that time winter isn't nearly over, the great winter buys are yet to come. January and February are the months when stores are stocking spring and summer goodies and desperately seeking to clear out the fall and winter items. August and September offer the best buys on spring and summer merchandise.

A common misimpression is that all the merchandise found at these end-of-season sales are the tackiest and most unpopular things. Wrong! Think about it. Whenever an item sells particularly well, it's re-stocked, often late enough in the season for some pieces to be left over and waiting for smart shoppers to pick up at the very best prices of the year.

And not all the best buys will be on the previous season's items. You see, as new merchandise pours in, department managers are scrambling to find space for stock, both in back and on the sales floor. Most stockrooms include a deep dark recess generally referred to as "the cave," which is where the remainder from the past season has ended up.

Let's say it's February. Most of the remaining stock will be winter items, but the treasures in "the cave" may be spring and summer leftovers. These will be added to the clearance goods and priced unbeatably low.

So with all that said, when is the best time to shop? Anytime. For the wise shopper, there is no day, time, or season that doesn't offer the possibility of fantastic bargains. Sure, there are certain times when great buys are at their most abundant; but every day of every week, the truly smart shopper can find those deep discounts.

How Deep Is Deep?

When I speak of deep discounts, how deep am I talking? *To me, if it's not at least 75% off, it's not on sale.*

Let me back up my claim. Since I'm on the road quite a bit, I'm always on the lookout for good packable fabrics, clothes that won't be wrinkled when they're unpacked from my luggage. In an upscale shop I recently found the perfect black knit T-shirt, something that can be used to really dress up, but that works just as well with a pair of jeans. The regular price? $36. The sale price? $9.

I'm not only talking about clothes. Larry and I have been redoing our house—furniture, flooring, wallpaper, everything. In my search for a sofa, I visited a furniture salvage store. I read that they had bought the entire stock of a manufacturing firm whose building was severely damaged during a tornado. I figured it was at least worth a look.

Sure enough, among some damaged, damp, and otherwise undesirable sofas sat a beautiful earthtone overstuffed beauty, complete with matching throw pillows and trimmed in a deep rich burgundy—exactly the colors I'd been hoping for. (You know that I prayed before making this trip!) Problem was, though, the sofa sat flat on the ground. The bun feet that should have been there were nowhere to be found. What to do?

Ask! When I flagged down a salesperson and inquired about the feet, he told me that they simply hadn't had time to attach them. That settled it—the sofa was mine. The price? $277.

I also have $60 sterling silver earrings I bought for $10; a $42 necklace I picked up for 99¢; a too too gorgeous 24x36 matted and framed print under glass for $18; an autographed copy of a bestselling book for $1; a $36 skirt I paid 65¢ for; and a zillion and one other impressive bargains.

You can be a God-pleasing, dollar-stretching consumer, too. These kinds of bargains are out there—it's simply a matter of knowing where and how to find them.

But I Don't Have Time to Shop for Bargains

The most common complaint I hear is that "I don't have time to shop." Yes, you do—you simply don't know how. That, my dear, is about to change, as I introduce you to:

The 10-Minute Shopping Rule.

We spend entirely too much time scoping out everything and focusing on nothing. Now, in any store, with the application of this simple shopping method, you can get in, find the bargains, and get out. It has three very important parts.

1. Get in. Begin your shopping trip with prayer. First Timothy 2:8 tells us: "in every place to pray." A more familiar passage, 1 Thessalonians 5:17, admonishes us to

"Pray without ceasing." I can't repeat this enough times: Our Heavenly Father is interested in every part of our lives.

Jesus Christ wants to participate with us. Invite Him. Ask Him to go with you and guide you to what you need and steer you clear of what you don't need. Ask Him to show you the very best buys.

In addition to these things I also ask the Lord to put blinders on me—to prevent me from seeing or wanting merchandise that isn't deep-discounted. After years of God shaping my perspective, I'm so oblivious to low- or no-discount items that the only way I see these are as part of the maze that will lead me to the bargains!

Now let me explain the 10-Minute Rule. I allow myself ten minutes to check out each floor of a store. If it's a huge one-level, I mentally divide the store into halves or quarters and allow ten minutes for each of these. If this concept is totally foreign to you, I'd recommend starting with ten minutes per department. Then I move to part 2 of the plan.

2. Find the bargains. These ten minutes are for one purpose: to look for the deep discounts. Unless they're using a bargain table or rack as a lure, departments invariably stick the best buys in the deepest recesses of their section, forcing you to walk all the way through the full-price merchandise in the hopes that you'll find something full price to spend your money on.

Make sure you go to the farthest corners of the department. Check the tags on hanging and folded merchandise even if no sale or clearance signs are in view. Sometimes the best buys aren't advertised at all.

Realize, too, that *sale* and *clearance* are relative terms. If it's less than normal retail, it could be considered either, and neither is necessarily the deepest discount. I've found better prices on sales racks than underneath clearance notices, and vice versa.

3. Get out. If there are no fabulous bargains, *walk out.* Go on to the next department or the next store, and don't waste any more time. The 10-Minute Rule is an excellent discipline to help you get the most out of your shopping time.

See? As prayed-up, conscientious Bargainomics® shoppers, you can breeze in, look for the clearance signs (which aren't always in place), turn over a few price tags, and walk away if you aren't spotting discounts of 75% or better. I'm telling you, this is so addictive! Once you find your first super discount, you'll feel like dancing in the aisle—and even if you skip that part, it will certainly be a good time to offer up thanksgiving and praise to the One who led you there.

And once you find those bargains, decide whether to

go ahead and make your purchases or to look in more stores in the area, making no purchases until you've checked out all the possibilities. As you decide, ask yourself: (1) Is this exactly what I want? (2) Will I find something better or cheaper elsewhere?

Whether you choose to camp out in one store or make the rounds first, once you locate deep discounts, if your timeframe is fairly open, take yourself off the clock and have at it. If your time is limited, though, decide how many stores you plan to visit, and allot your time accordingly.

Let's Review

1. The Occasions List. Don't leave home without it.

A. By doing your Christmas and other occasion shopping all year long, you'll discover the wonderful freedom that comes from spreading the expense throughout the year.

B. When Christmas arrives, you'll be free of much of the associated stress and pressure.

C. If you get the "urge to shop," the list will help you put those urges to a better purpose.

2. Don't be afraid to ask. The worst thing they can tell you is "no."

A. Ask for boxes and related goodies every time you shop, even when you intend to keep the items for yourself.

B. At home, box your items and pencil recipients' names on the bottoms of the boxes. Keep everything in one location designated for gift storage.

3. If it's not 75% off, it's not on sale.

A. Pray as you shop. Ask the Lord to lead you to the very best buys.

B. Trust Him to show you these bargains; resist the temptation to settle for less than the super deep discounts.

4. The 10-Minute Shopping Rule.

A. *Get in:* Pray. Allot yourself ten minutes to scope out a floor or department.

B. *Find the bargains:* If you don't, walk away. If you do, decide whether to shop now or check other spots first.

C. *Get out:* Once you've grabbed up the bargains, leave; but first, make sure you pick up boxes, etc., if available.

Where to Shop

Retail stores. Retail stores can be excellent bargain sources. As we've already discussed, the trick is knowing where to look and not being afraid to ask if there is a clearance or sale section.

At a home improvement store I found an entire section of shelving dedicated to clearance merchandise. I brought home a simple 3-light chandelier—just what I'd been looking for—for only $9. At a jeweler's, I found $89 earrings in a clearance case for $19. There is pretty much no type of merchandise I haven't been able to find at super deep discounts while retail shopping.

Discount stores. Some stores specialize in buying overstocks, discontinued items, and such. Sure, you may have to wade through some less desirable merchandise in order to find your bargain goodie, but your stop might be well worth your effort.

During our remodeling frenzy I found name-brand 5x8 rugs—not seconds, not damaged—that had ended up in a discount store for $19 each. The manufacturer's tags were still attached with the regular retail price of $200.

"Dollar" stores receive shipments of all sorts of items, all of which can be purchased for $1 each. I've bought CDs, movies, makeup, personal care products, silk flowers, paper goods, vases and other knickknacks, grocery items, and even hose and socks.

Outlets. There are so many places calling themselves "outlets" nowadays that it's hard to tell the real thing from the phony. Many manufacturers regularly sell their goods at their outlet stores for one-half the stickered price. In some cases this is a good buy. In others, it's a joke.

As with every part of your life, it goes back to being an intelligent steward. Have a general idea of the value of merchandise. Don't assume that half off a pair of $48 jeans

($24) is a good deal simply because you're getting half off an already inflated price tag.

Remember, too, that you may or may not be getting "seconds"—merchandise that in some way didn't pass as first quality. The flaw may be completely unnoticeable, somewhat noticeable but something you can live with, or so obvious as to make the item undesirable. The important thing is to look the item over from top to bottom.

When it comes to electronics, power tools, small appliances, and such, these are sometimes factory-reconditioned items. In most cases the full warranty still applies, but ask to be certain. And read the box or label to see what parts and accessories are included and make sure all these are accounted for.

Probably my all-time best outlet buy was in early February at a well-known dinnerware manufacturer's. I'd wanted a new set of dishes—I had collected my old set piece by piece as part of a grocery store's promotion. On the sidewalk sale were the dishes of my dreams, at $4 per place setting and $3 for each serving piece. My serving for 12 cost me $65. The retail price for all those pieces was over $800.

I'm telling you, ladies, I'm not a remarkable shopper, nor am I remarkable in other ways. But I serve a totally remarkable God who cares so much about His children that it even matters to Him about the dishes I like! He cares about every single part of my life and He gladly guides and accompanies me on every decision, when I invite Him to guide me.

How hard is it for you to find a really good buy? How hard is it for you to even find the sort of item you have in mind? Have you tried asking for help?

Jesus told His disciples, "the Comforter [Counselor, Helper, Advocate, Intercessor, Strengthener, Standby] . . . I will send Him to you" (John 16:7 AMP). Child of God, your Comforter, your Counselor, your Helper, stands ready to help you shop like the sharpest, most selective consumer ever possible. When have you invited Him along?

Consignment shops. Not everyone is familiar with consignment shopping, so let me explain. A consignment shop is a store where an individual can take his/her unwanted goods to be resold. Some shops accept only clothing and accessories; others specialize in furniture, some take just about anything. But all work on a commission basis, with the store retaining as their fee a percentage of the sales price of each item.

Like other shops, the variety, selection, pricing, and quality can vary tremendously. But with very few exceptions, items in consignment shops are gently used, in good condition, and reasonably priced.

Many stores indicate on the sales tag the date the merchandise was received. Then as time passes and the item remains unsold, the price decreases, usually on a scale of

0–30 days (tagged price); 31–60 days (generally 25–50% off); 61–90 (generally 50–75% off). Rarely will a shop retain merchandise longer than 90 days.

Items in different date brackets (and therefore, the associated discounts) aren't usually separated, so in most cases, you'll just have to look at the dating on the tags. Thankfully, though, lots of these shops color-code tags so that specific colors indicate the timeframe during which the item was received. Once you've figured out which color indicates which dates, you'll know which items carry the best discounts.

Other shops do separate items that have been around a while and they are eager to move. Look for these as in shopping anywhere else—they're usually stuck in the farthest recesses and corners.

Thrift shops. These include familiar names like Goodwill and Salvation Army stores, but many thrift shops are owned by individual churches, community programs, and other non-profit and not-for-profit organizations. I love these stores!

You'll rarely find a thrift shop that's as neat and clean as a consignment shop, but trust me—wading through a little bit of clutter can net you some fabulous bargains. It's just going to take a little trial and error to learn which shops are worthwhile and which you may as well not waste your time on.

Home Shopping. Nowadays marketing gets us

from every angle, from the catalog in the mailbox to the home shopping television stations, from telephone solicitors to Internet shopping. How can we do any of these and still avoid credit or other unwise spending?

Unless you are 100% disciplined to pay your credit card balance in full each time you receive a statement, please, please, please don't use a credit card to do any shopping. Take no chances. Satan is eager to bring you down, child of God. Don't let him get a foot in the door through credit debt.

Some catalogs have excellent clearance sections. Even the home shopping networks offer some pretty impressive closeouts now and then. In either case, make sure that the shipping expense doesn't defeat the good price of the merchandise. Too, be certain of what you're ordering and be aware of the company's return policy—you don't want to end up needlessly paying return shipping and you sure don't want to be stuck with unwanted or incorrect merchandise.

How do you order without using credit? Mail a check or money order along with an order form or handwritten order. Make sure you include the appropriate amount for the merchandise plus shipping and handling.

Online shopping. As a professional night owl, I do a lot of late night Internet shopping. And honey, let me tell you, it can be addictive. But it can also be very rewarding.

For example, tucked away in the hardest-to-spot

region of many stores' home pages lies the Clearance Zone. From LifeWay Christian Book Stores (www.lifewaystores.com) to Walmart (www.walmart.com), there are bargains galore out in cyberspace. The trick is not only to find the Web site, but to then find the clearance sections.

One good way to find a Web site is to guess. If the store's name is Podunk, then there's a high probability that their site is: *www.podunk.com.* But of course, there's no guarantee that there is an existing site or that this is the one you're looking for. But it's a way to start.

Another way is to use a search engine, which is a kind of cyberspace train that goes out and loads up the info you're looking for and brings it back to you. A couple of engines that may be familiar to you are www.yahoo.com and www.about.com.

I prefer what is sometimes referred to as a mega-search engine, which is basically a train onto which all the other engines can be hooked together and sent out to return with a huge load of information from any number of regular search engines. My personal favorites are www.dogpile.com (the name's not pretty, but the results are top-notch) and www.cyber411.com.

So how great are the bargains out there? Take LifeWay. Among my many LifeWay finds, I've landed children's books for under a dollar and beautiful coffee table books ($15+ in the real stores) for two bucks. But in order to find their clearance goodies, I had to expand their site to fill my entire screen. Once I'd done that, thar she blew, way over in the far upper right.

eBay and other auction sites. Here's where you can save—and spend—a fortune. eBay is the largest and oldest online auction service where buyers can bid on and sellers can sell anything imaginable and then some. My purchases have included everything from clothing to camera equipment.

If you've never tried online bidding, you might want to visit the site and click on "search" to locate items you might be interested in. The rest of the process is fairly self-explanatory. Each seller's listed item is described in detail and usually includes a photo or photos. The date and time that particular auction ends is noted.

The opening bid price and other details, including current bid price, are listed. When you place a bid, you are entering into a contract that you are obligated to complete, should you win the auction. You set a maximum amount and the system automatically bids for you each time someone tops your bid, right up to your maximum.

You don't have to worry about paying more than you'd planned—once your maximum bid is surpassed by another bidder, you're out of the running. You will, however, receive an e-mail message letting you know that you need to bid again if you're willing to go higher on your offering price.

Two other very important pieces of information are

also included with each listing: the seller's accepted methods of payment and shipping charges. Personally, I prefer to stick with sellers who accept personal checks, cashier's checks, and money orders rather than those who require the use of a credit card.

I'm also very careful to check the amount the seller requires as a shipping charge. When no specifics are given, I contact the seller (the how-to for this is also provided on the listing) and ask what the shipping to my zip code would be. This might not sound all that important, but I've seen listings with shipping charges of $15 and more.

Final Words

I came up with the 75% rule and the 10-minute rule for retail shopping, but I've found these apply as well in many shopping situations. The more I learn about trusting the Lord to guide my shopping, the more I'm convicted of the importance of stretching my dollars and using my shopping time wisely.

Determine in advance to make a quick sweep of things. Once you do, you'll have begun disciplining yourself as a Bargainomics® shopper. Look around. Check a few prices. If what you see indicates less than satisfactory pricing or merchandise, don't waste any further time. Leave and save that time for elsewhere.

The more we look at smart consumerism, the more we'll see that *discipline* is the key. Have you ever stopped to think about that word? It comes from the same root word as *disciple*. A disciple is a learner, a follower of a particular teaching. Discipline is what keeps a disciple following the instructions of his teacher.

Remember when you were in grade school? My third grade teacher was Miss Flossie. She insisted that her students sit up prim and proper in their seats, and we were never to talk unless directed to do so.

One day I decided I had news too earth-shattering to wait for recess. While Miss Flossie wrote on the blackboard, I eased around in my desk seat, got on my knees, and leaned over to tell the girl behind me my urgent info. Next thing I remember, my bottom was firmly whacked with Miss Flossie's notorious wooden paddle and my face turned as red as my bottom probably did!

You see, the brighter kids understood that the best way to learn from Miss Flossie's rules were to follow them; in other words, they were disciplined by *knowing* the rules rather than by breaking them and learning from the consequences. I, on the other hand, was unwilling to be disciplined simply by obeying the rules—which is exactly what made Miss Flossie's intervention necessary.

A smart disciple wants to discipline herself, that is, choose to obey/follow what she has been taught. A foolish disciple learns through disobedience and the subsequent discipline resulting from it, whether from natural consequences or enforcement by a teacher.

It boils down to this: smart disciple, fast learner; foolish disciple, slow learner. It's your conscious and willful decision. Which category do you choose to be in? Our Teacher desires and blesses obedient disciples, and He loves the wayward ones enough to let them learn from their mistakes.

The Father has given you and me one lifetime. How much of that life is self-disciplined, disciplined through the results of disobedience, or dealt with through the Father's degrees of discipline is entirely up to you.

As a believer in Jesus Christ, have you accepted the fact that all you have and are belongs to Him? Remember 1 Corinthians 6:19–20 (NIV): "You are not your own; you were bought at a price." Honor Him with how you live.

Chapter 4

Let's Start with the Basics—Food

"I say to you, do not be worried about your life, as to what you will eat or what you will drink."
—Matthew 6:25

"One should eat to live, and not live to eat."
—Molière, *Le Bourgeois Gentilhomme*

"There's a thin person inside of me trying to get out, but I keep her sedated with chocolate."
—shop window in Fairhope, Alabama

ood! A subject near and dear to my heart. For many
of us, food is more than nourishment, more than
sustenance—it is a source of both comfort and
entertainment. And to a point, there's nothing wrong with
that. What most of us struggle with, though, is ignoring
Scriptures such as: "Eat only what you need" (Proverbs
25:16).

Truth is, most of us are food-obsessed, whether we
overeat or not. Larry claims that I choose vacation desti-
nations according to the food. He has gone so far as to say
that I can tell people more about where and what we ate
than about what we saw!

But any way you slice it, we spend an incredible
amount of money on food. What to do? Quit eating out?
Stick to bread and water? Aren't there some ways to
reduce our expenses without taking all the fun out of
America's favorite pastime? Absolutely!

Dining Out

1. "Buy 1, Get 1 Free." Many restaurants offer specials on specific days of the week. For example, at a
Mexican restaurant near my home, on Mondays two can
dine for the price of one, paying for the higher-priced meal
and getting the second meal at no charge. Not a bad deal
just for eating out on the right day, is it?

2. Lunch instead of dinner. Most restaurants that are

open for lunch and dinner offer lunch items at lower prices than dinner. My example here is a local Chinese eatery. Most lunches sell for around $4.95 and include soup, egg roll, and main dish. Dinners, which include only slightly larger portions, average $8.95, with soup and egg roll extra.

3. Love those coupons! Newspapers and junk mail are terrific sources of instant discounts. If you don't regularly subscribe to a daily newspaper, it may be worth your while to buy Sunday and Wednesday editions just for the coupons (more on coupons later in this chapter).

When you do use any type of coupon, make sure you read the fine print—many are limited to specific locations, days, times, dates, and items. Too, once you've eaten, check your bill to be certain the coupon value has been deducted.

4. Don't forget your discounts. You may be pleasantly surprised how many discounts you're eligible for. Some restaurants offer these for AAA and other travel club members. Others have their own senior discounts, occasionally for as low as 50 years of age!

5. Kids eat free. This can be both a positive and negative. While a number of restaurants offer "Kids Eat Free" days or even as an everyday deal, you may still come out better dining elsewhere. A steak and seafood eatery serves up meals with an average entree price of $12. Let's look at a family of four: If two adults are dining, that's $24, plus tax and gratuity, even if the two children get their meals at no cost. OOPS! What about drinks? These are rarely included, so let's tack on another $6 for these, shall we? Now our total has shot past $35.

Another restaurant offers entrees at $8 each with kids' meals (drinks included) at $1.89. Let's figure this one up: adding together the parents' meals and drinks, kids' meals, tax, and gratuity, this family will spend less than $30.

6. Split the entree. The Apple Barn in Sevierville, Tennessee serves up delicious home-sized portions of great country cooking. All their entrees are large. For instance, their mouth-watering fried chicken entree includes 2 breasts plus mounded bowls of veggies and piping hot bread. For a nominal additional charge, these nice folks will split the entree and allow both diners to feast on the goodies.

An Italian restaurant Larry and I like offers a three-pasta platter, and he and I can both eat to our heart's content. We simply order an extra salad and request an extra plate. Then we kick back and indulge in steamy fresh breadsticks and salad. When the entree is brought out, we put half on the extra plate and enjoy a fantastic meal at a very reasonable charge.

Don't be embarrassed to ask about splitting an entree. Why on earth pay for or waste food unnecessarily? Not all restaurants offer this option, but as you'll hear me repeat over and over, it never hurts to ask because the worst thing they can tell you is "no"!

7. Let's share! If portions are large or your appetite isn't, there isn't a thing wrong with sharing one plate. However, let your waiter know this is what you intend to do and request an extra plate. In a few rare cases, I know of restaurants charging for the extra empty plate. My advice, should you run across one of these, is to in the future take your business elsewhere.

In defense of restaurant policies, however, let me remind you that sharing is never an acceptable practice when dining at an "all-you-care-to-eat" or other buffet. Stealing is stealing, and when you pay for one person at one of these restaurants, you're declaring that only one person will be eating from the buffet—never, never, never share buffet meals.

8. What's *not* on the menu? Daily specials and other offerings are frequently available if you'll only ask. Lloyd's Restaurant on Highway 280 below Birmingham has been a popular spot for many years. One unadvertised dish, known as "The Sheriff's Special" (named after the officers who first requested it), features a combo of half servings of their delicious barbecue pork and first-rate hamburger steak.

Since discovering "The Sheriff's Special," I've learned that it's often possible to get half-servings of more than one entree rather than having to stick to a single choice. Too, there are often daily specials that your waiter might fail to announce. These can include specialty dishes and lower-priced offerings.

9. 'Tis the season. Since winter is the Alabama Gulf Coast's off-season for tourists, lots of spots offer incredible meal deals, particularly at lunchtime. Some people who take full advantage of this are the "snowbirds" (northerners who come south until warmer weather). If you live in or visit any vacation area during its off-season, keep your eyes peeled for these bargains.

10. Guess-timate. This may be a "duh" thing to most of you, but let me urge you to "guess-timate" your total bill so you'll have a good idea what you'll be paying. Cashiers or waiters may inadvertently misprice, leave off coupons, or fail to credit discounts. If your total is higher than anticipated, ask for an explanation or re-count.

Take-out Dining

Even when funds are really tight, you still want to avoid that time in the kitchen, don't you? That's why drive-thru lines are packed with people after work. Here are some tips to help with take-out dining:

• If the choice is between eating inside the restaurant or using the drive-thru or take-out service, by all means, use the drive-thru or take-out. Using our same family of four (I keep using them—let's give them a name! How about Sherry for the mom; Larry, the dad; and Moe and Curly, the kiddies), let's look at an example:

Cutie's Cuisine offers a dinner special for only $5.99 per plate. If your foursome eats at the restaurant, even choosing to drink water, you're looking at an additional $3 to cover the tip. Do the math. If you take out instead of dine in once a week, in a year's time, *you'd save $156*.

• Here's another scenario: Spiffy Burgers offers a burger, fries, and drink combo for $3.99. Guess what? You can buy the burger and fries for $2.98. Unless there are clearly defined savings, skip the combo and serve your own beverage (iced tea or flavored drink mixes cost only pennies a serving) at home. Your annual savings, even after allowing for home beverage expense? *More than $200*. I'll drink to that!

Now that I have your Bargainomics® brain cells thinking in drink mode, let me toss you a tidbit to absorb: If you will simply forego beverages when you eat out—

that is, opt for good ol' H2O, as in water—not only do you save the cost of the actual beverages, you save the related taxes and increased gratuities. You also discipline yourself and your family to drink a healthy calorie-free liquid.

"But," you protest, "we'd much rather drink something else!" Let me put it this way: First, what are the savings? A family of four eating out once every week can save enough money to take a nice Bargainomics® vacation: *more than $350 a year*. Second, this is a great way to teach your children to participate in family decisions and learn good money management skills.

In other words, try it this way: "Hey, kids, if you had to choose between a weekend at [insert a favorite spot here] or a [insert a beverage name here], which would it be?" Your youngsters won't have to be honor roll students to make this choice!

Once you've gotten their attention, make them the offer: water at restaurants and the savings in a vacation fund or business as usual. You may even want to exercise a little parental authority on this and insist on their cooperation.

But be sure you keep your word. Tuck each meal's "savings" into a special envelope or savings account and, when a sufficient amount has been accumulated, put it to use as promised. The resulting reward will be great family fun and a memorable learning experience for everyone.

Home Dining

If you're impressed at the number of ways to cut corners eating out, just wait until you discover the savings that exist for dining at home! One of the easiest and biggest here is once again:

Beverages! If you're in the habit of buying name-brand soft drinks (soda, pop, cola—whatever you want to call it), think on this: If you're buying three 3-liter drinks per week, you're spending around *$280 per year*. If you're buying only two 12-packs of name-brand cans, your cost just jumped to *$440*.

But even if you're buying generics, you're still spending quite a little bundle. What about the alternatives? Water, of course, is the healthiest and least expensive drink. Consider, too, that recent reports have shown that regulations for city water services are far stricter than those governing bottling companies. If you're paying for bottled water, you may be throwing away money on poorer quality water. Consider installing water filters on your kitchen faucet and icemaker line.

Generic flavored drink mix, using your own sugar, costs only pennies per glass. My current cost for a half-gallon is about *29¢*. My iced tea, sweetened as we Southerners love it, costs about *13¢* per half-gallon.

Food! For most of us, time is stretched to its limits already, so time in the kitchen is something we definitely want to keep at a minimum. But consider these points:

1. With a little effort, mealtimes can become the best family time of the day. (Granted, if you have toddlers this probably won't be the case!) And family time is precious, even to teens who would never admit it.

2. Preparing food at home makes money available for things like vacations and other special treats. With today's appliances and resources, cooking is not the chore it used to be. And if you involve your family in preparation, even this time can be used to teach, listen, and be together.

3. Smells are our strongest memories. I can close my eyes right now and recall my Big Mama Woodward's big ol' biscuits—how the steam would gush out as I opened one and melted farm-fresh pale yellow butter on it. Good smells attract. And a fragrant kitchen can bring pleasure, savings, and even better communication to your household.

When to Shop

Ever wonder why the amount you spend on food is astronomical? For many of us there's one reason. In order for any plan to work, guess what? *There has to be one!* Knowing when, where, and how to shop will save you time, money, and energy. Most importantly, it's one very vital way we can honor our Lord with wise stewardship.

Unless this is something you enjoy, why spend your Saturday at the grocery store? If you're an early riser, consider buying groceries and bringing them home before going to work. Or why not make the stop on the way home from work? Nowadays many grocers are open 24 hours a day, which gives you multiple opportunities to shop during less crowded hours. If you choose a less-crowded time to shop, you'll feel less pressured to rush, and you'll be more likely to make wise decisions.

Feed me! Shopping while you're hungry makes everything look good, and you're sure to spend more. Choose a time when your tummy is full and food is not so attractive.

Without the children. If you have youngsters at home, find a time when you can shop without their company. Not only will they distract you and slow your mission, they'll bombard you with requests for extra goodies.

Where to shop

Choose a store in close proximity to your other activities such as dry cleaners, bank, etc. This way, with proper planning, you can make one stop that will take care of all your regular needs.

Be price-smart, too, which may take a bit of exploration. But you'll find most stores are higher on some things and lower on others and, in most cases, it wouldn't pay to hop store-to-store scooping up lower-priced items.

This is especially true of most places' weekly specials.

Think big! Many grocers include an aisle stocked with commercial-sized canned goods such as beans and corn. Compared with the price of smaller serving containers, these can be a real bargain. At home, open and separate reasonable portions into storage containers; then freeze until needed.

Non-perishables. Small discount stores such as Dollar General, Family Dollar, Fred's, and such are consistently lower on prices for cleaning items, laundry and dishwasher detergent, softener sheets, plastic wrap, aluminum foil, paper towels, etc. Most of these also carry a fair stock of seasoning mixes and spices that are impressively cheaper than most regular grocers.

Bakery outlets. Bread stores and bakery outlets are great places to pick up bread, buns, packaged rolls, lunch cakes, and more at remarkably good prices, often 50–75% less than grocers. Too, all these items freeze well, so you can stock up when you recognize a real bargain.

Bent 'n' Dent stores. Bent 'n' dent or salvage stores are another super-savings possibility. These goods include damaged merchandise such as dented cans and bent boxes, but they also include unblemished items from the same shipment, as well as merchandise which is nearing or past its expiration date. Select only those products that are within their pre-expiration dating and avoid severely bent cans or packages that have been torn and resealed. With a little extra inspecting, you can stock up at substantial savings.

How to Shop

Plan a weekly menu. Painful though this may sound, even having a general idea of what you plan to prepare during the week means less time at your grocer's and less time in the kitchen—and less money wasted on unnecessary purchases.

There are scads of dishes that can be prepared easily and quickly. (A few recipes are listed at the end of this chapter.) I was appalled to see a one-box casserole-style meal on my grocer's shelf for almost $4. Inside were two small cans (mixed vegetables and boneless chicken) plus a small package of biscuit mix. The box claimed the prepared dish would feed four. Of course, it didn't say four what, so I suspect it meant four ants.

Anyway, I figured up the cost of the same three items purchased separately: $2.75. And the resulting dish would have been at least 25% larger.

Make a shopping list. Without a doubt the most expensive way to buy groceries is to dash in every other day or two to pick up a few items. Invariably, when you read the total for your meager purchases, you leave wearing that stunned "deer-in-the-headlights" look and staring at your empty wallet.

Set a regular day to buy groceries. Allot a

specific amount and stick to it. Budgeting (also known as a spending plan) is **not** an ugly word. Inventory your household needs before heading out so as to eliminate additional trips or stops.

Don't be afraid to ask. (There's that phrase again!) The people who work in the produce, meat, and bakery departments will be glad to tell you if there is a particular time or day of the week when you're most likely to find reduced items on hand. Most stores regularly date items and discount them once their freshness date has expired. Don't worry, I've been buying reduced foods for years and have never had a bad experience. Just look the product over as you should when buying full-price items. How much can you save? On most items, you can expect discounts of 30–75%.

Seasonal savings. I find at least one or two bargain items almost every time I shop, but logically, there are some times that are better than others for scarfing up the best buys. For example, turkeys and hams are often overstocked for holiday shoppers. Since these will easily keep (fully frozen) six months to a year, these are often terrific post-holiday bargains—and can be legally consumed on non-holidays! When fruits are in season stock is highest and overages are most likely. You might also want to ask a store manager when inventory is done—many slow-moving items are discounted and deleted during this time.

About coupons. Coupons can be useful tools in

getting the most for your dollars, but don't focus on them to the point that you fail to check other products. Recently I clipped a 75¢-off coupon for a spaghetti sauce. When I took it to the store and compared the prices, I discovered that this particular product was so expensive that, even without a coupon, several other brands would cost less money.

Coupons are advertising. As basic as this may sound, think about it a minute. Coupons draw your attention to the items they represent and encourage you to take advantage of their "savings." Use coupons for products you were already planning to buy. Don't be lured into buying something simply because you have a coupon for the product.

Pray. Are your groceries important enough for you to pray about? Look back at the first page of this chapter and see what Jesus had to say. When it comes to any kind of decision, we do one of two things: worry or pray.

Think of it this way. *Anything we don't entrust to God is not His.* The Lord will never take what you do not freely give. I think one of Satan's greatest deceptions among Christians is to make us think that we shouldn't bother our Father with trivialities. And as long as he can fool us into thinking that, we will always have those "little" areas of our lives that are not fully entrusted to the Savior.

What did the apostle Paul tell us? "In everything . . .

let your requests be made known to God" (Philippians 4:6). Our Heavenly Father most assuredly knows and understands our need and desire for good food, as well as the time constraints of our busy everyday lives.

There is no area of your life in which the Lord does not want to be involved. There is no area of your life where He does not want to be in control. Is eating a part of your life? Then just as surely is obtaining those provisions. Ask God to guide you to seek out the best and healthiest buys for your family. He stands ready and willing to help you.

Learn to Love Your Kitchen

If I may stand on my soapbox for a moment or two, I'd like to comment on the current state of collapse in the average kitchen. It seems that in our all-out effort to ditch the June Cleaver image, some women have gone to the opposite extreme—and I do mean extreme!

When speaking with many women today I hear, "Oh, I don't cook." Or "I let Johnny handle all that." Puh-lease! Does refusing to learn your way around the kitchen make you more a woman of today? Hardly.

Nowadays any person, male or female, who has the intelligence to open a can or push a button can cook and cook well. And it doesn't even require a fully-equipped kitchen to get the job done. Here are some tips to help you learn to love your kitchen.

1. Invest in a toaster oven. My toaster oven was purchased for $7 at a local thrift store (with their standard 30-day warranty, of course) and has a large enough capacity to cook up to four servings of most foods. Why crank up a 220-volt oven when this little 110-volt beauty can do the job just as well?

2. Break out the crock-pot. At another thrift store I invested $3.88 in a large-capacity crock-pot with the lift-out crock (30-day warranty included). This handy gadget makes it easy to whip up stews, soups, dried beans, roasts, and oodles of other dishes. And a properly prepared crock-pot can be safely used unattended all day or night.

3. Cook twice as much as you need. Each time you cook, make enough for two meals. Serve half and freeze the other half to be served at a later date. (Masking tape makes great inexpensive freezer tape. Always label and date items you plan to freeze.)

4. Save those leftovers. Many leftover foods, even in small quantities, can be frozen and kept as ingredients for soups, casseroles, or other dishes. Once you get into the habit of saving "a little of this 'n that," you'll discover it's really nice to have these extra additives on hand.

Add It Up

If you've taken the time to look back over the dollar figures in this chapter, you'll see that the virtually painless adjustments mentioned total somewhere in the neighborhood of $1,000 a year. As clearly as our smaller decisions affect our pocketbooks, they also affect the way we make our more important decisions. Until we get a firm grasp on that concept, it's far too easy to justify spending too much money on eating out, fast food, and quick-fix products.

Ephesians 6:11–17 talks about putting on the "full armor of God" (Ephesians 6:11). If you read on to verse 16, we're told that it's the "shield of faith with which you will be able to extinguish all the flaming arrows of the evil one." In biblical war-times, an enemy would light an arrow before shooting it at his opponent. Properly worn armor had no "chink" in which the arrow could lodge and hurt the soldier, but poorly- or partially-worn armor could be breached with one of these flaming missiles, causing serious harm or even death.

You see, even the tiniest pieces of that armor were vital. Even the minute details of its makeup were critical to the safety of the soldier within. We are to be clothed likewise. How did those soldiers fend off the arrows? With the "shield of faith." If you have the faith to trust God for anything, then why not trust Him for all things? Ask Him to guide your spending for food and groceries.

Recipes to Get You Started

Here are a few recipes to get you started on the road to cooking pleasure and confidence.

Cheesy Carrot Casserole

3 cups of sliced carrots

¼ cup bread crumbs (make your own by putting a slice of bread in your food processor)

2 tablespoons margarine

2 tablespoons finely chopped onion

1 tablespoon light brown sugar

¼ cup evaporated milk

½ cup shredded cheese (extra sharp cheddar is delicious in this)

Preheat oven to 350 degrees; meanwhile, in the microwave, steam the carrots in a tad of salted water, just until tender; drain. Spray a casserole dish with nonstick spray and set aside. Add to the carrots all the ingredients except the cheese; mix well. Top with cheese, spread into the casserole dish, and bake for 30 minutes.

Sweetheart Cake

2 cans (20 ounces each) cherry (or other fruit) pie filling
1 box white cake mix
1 cup chopped pecans
2 sticks of margarine
(I never said this was low fat!)

Lightly spray a 9x13 baking pan with nonstick spray. Pour pie filling evenly along bottom to cover. Sprinkle dry cake mix on top of the pie filling. Top with pecans. Thinly slice margarine and dot all over the top. Bake at 350 degrees for 30 to 40 minutes, or until lightly browned.

Chicken & Rice Soup

2 cups of uncooked rice
½ cup milk
1 can cream of chicken soup
1 pound uncooked chicken
salt and pepper to taste

Boil your pound of chicken, saving the broth. Remove the skin and bone, and cut the meat into small cubes or chunks. Put the meat back into the broth and set it aside. Next, cook your rice. Use low-cost long-cooking rice (takes about 15 minutes) and cook per package directions—finished product will give you 4 cups of rice. Add the cooked rice to the chicken and broth, stir in the milk and cream of chicken soup, and mix thoroughly. Simmer until thoroughly heated, salt and pepper to taste, and there you have it! Soup thickness is a personal preference, so add more water to thin; drain or simmer longer to cook away unwanted water. Freeze leftovers for a second delicious meal.

Sweet 'n' Sour Green Beans

2 cups cooked green beans
1 finely chopped onion
3 tablespoons light brown sugar
1 tablespoon margarine
4 teaspoons white or apple cider
  vinegar
4 slices of bacon, cooked and
  crumbled

While the beans are piping hot, add the raw onion; stir in. (Make sure the beans aren't too "soupy;" if there's too much liquid, spoon out and discard a bit.) In the microwave, heat the brown sugar, margarine, and vinegar until hot; blend well and pour mixture over beans. Top with crumbled bacon and serve.

Chapter 5

Let's Start with the Basics— Clothing

*"I say to you, do not be worried about your life . . .
as to what you will put on."*

—Matthew 6:25

*"Little lamb, who made thee?
Dost thou know who made thee,
. . . Gave thee clothing of delight,
Softest clothing, woolly, bright."*

—**William Blake,** *The Lamb*

Whenever I look through a catalog or fashion magazine, I am absolutely thunderstruck by the price tags on the outfits. A pair of casual slacks for $178. A simple pullover top for $120. Sandals at $235 a pair. Casual and simple, my eyeball! Who would pay that kind of money for an outfit!?!

You're probably right there with me, aren't you? "Yeah, that's right. Those prices are ridiculous!" But I'd guess most of you very easily invest $100 or more in an outfit by the time you figure in shoes and accessories. Ladies, this is unnecessary.

Shopping is shopping, and the same know-how that gets you the best buys on foods will also help you reel in the bargains on clothing: knowing when, where, and how to shop.

Hopefully the information in chapter three has you pumped full of shopping savvy, but if you're anything like me, shopping for clothing is important enough to warrant a separate space of its own. For starters, let me remind you to:

Stop and Think

Once you find those bargains, decide whether to go ahead and make your purchases or to look in other area stores first so you'll be aware of all the possibilities. Prayerfully ask yourself: (1) Is this exactly what I want? (2) Will I find something better or cheaper elsewhere?

Whether you choose to camp out in one store or make the rounds first, once you locate deep discounts, if your timeframe is fairly open, take yourself off the clock and have at it. If your time is limited, though, decide how many stores you plan to hit, and allot your time accordingly.

Shop By the Rules

When buying for yourself, try clothing on. Avoid the urge to pick up a good buy that "will fit fine once I've lost a few pounds." *If it doesn't fit now, you don't need it now.* Abiding by this discipline will save you many a grief in having to return and exchange items.

Know the store's return policy, especially if you're buying an item as a gift. In most cases returned sales merchandise is treated the same as full-priced items. But be aware that some stores don't refund money, but only issue in-store credit. A rare few state no return or refund on clearance merchandise.

Wherever you shop, you'll find you have a limited time to return something: sometimes 10 days, sometimes 30, sometimes more. Make sure you know these rules and abide by them so you're never stuck with an item.

Fear No Store

Don't assume that any shop is out of your league. Even the trendiest upscale shops can offer some of the most fabulous bargains. A regular-priced outfit in one store I dearly love can easily set a person back $400, but brave soul that I've become, I marched in there and asked, "Do you have any clearance merchandise?" The very sweet saleslady immediately directed me to a discreet little armoire tucked away (naturally) in the far back corner.

Ah! Sweet music to my ears as she informed me, "Any item in this cabinet is always $10 or under." I am now the proud owner of an exquisite $88 pullover. Yes indeed, upscale boutiques can be wonderful bargain sources when you prayerfully approach your shopping excursion.

Remember, ask about clearance items. Then if these are still too extravagant, you're free to walk out the door. But if you don't try, you'll never know, will you—and you might miss out on an incredible, low-cost new goodie.

Can We Talk?

I want to share the condensed version of a very long story. Years ago I met a young woman, a divorced single parent, who came in to clean the office I was working in. As Wanda (not her real name) and I got to know each other, I was astounded to learn that she was college-educated. She said she'd tried finding better work, but had never been able to land anything else.

Mother Hen to the rescue! Some time later I learned of a job opening where I worked, one that required no experience, included paid on-the-job training, and offered tremendous opportunities for advancement. I bee-lined to Wanda, told her I could set up an interview, and urged her to dress her very best when she came.

I learned a valuable lesson that day as this buxom sweetie nervously came to my office en route to the interview. She was clad in a form-fitting sweater, short leather skirt, and fishnet hose, with 4-inch stiletto heels on her feet. Most of you are probably picturing exactly what I was—she looked like she was seeking a very different kind of employment than the job I was sending her to.

I parked Wanda in my office and dashed to the person who was to interview her. I explained that I was the cause for her unorthodox dress, that she was merely trying, albeit wrongfully, to make a good impression. I pleaded her case, told him that if he would overlook her appearance, I was sure she would eagerly accept any suggestions that he made regarding normal office attire and that she would, in spite of appearances, be a dependable and trustworthy employee.

Blessedly, this man agreed. Wanda enjoyed a long and happy career with her new employer.

I'm here to tell you that like the old saying, "The clothes make the man," they also make the woman. You can make an unforgettably good or bad impression simply by the way you dress.

So how do I dress? Another familiar saying comes to mind: "When in Rome . . ." Make sure your clothing fits the occasion. Too, we need to be careful not to assume that we know what's appropriate. When in doubt, ask. Ask a friend; look at the godly women you admire and see what they wear and where they wear it. And when you can't find clear guidance, you're much better off to slightly overdress rather than under.

But I can only afford so many clothes . . . Church, work, home, social occasions, errands, vacations, holidays. What's a girl to do? With a hundred different occasions in mind, do you really need a hundred different outfits to get the job done? Nope, not even close. Which brings up a travel story of my own.

In doing travel writing, I sometimes get invitations to participate in press or media tours, trips sponsored by a particular city or visitors bureau for the purpose of drawing in writers and showing them what a great place they have for us to write about. We're flown in, chauffeured around, taken to the finest hotels, restaurants, and events, and expected to dress appropriately for each step of the itinerary.

The more I travel, the less I like packing. To help me travel light, I have whittled my wardrobe down to some very versatile pieces. On this particular trip, though, we were doing a lot of walking every day, then having very dressy evening events.

Not a problem. I'd brought along a simple black sleeveless ankle-length knit dress, my $11 absolute fashion necessity. I tell you, these new fabrics are heaven-sent! They're the perfect travel duds: roll them up and they unroll unwrinkled and ready to wear; hand wash and hang over the tub and they'll drip dry and be wrinkle-free in only a few hours.

So, on a 5-day tour, I brought along this one dress for evenings and more casual items to wear during the day. On Monday night, we dined at a beautiful four-star restaurant. I wore my black dress topped with a multi-colored cotton jacket. Tuesday we were off to the opera. For that, I topped the dress with a black bolero style jacket trimmed in elaborate silver and gold braiding. (Of course, I accessorized nicely and differently with each outfit.)

Wednesday evening was another fancy dinner. This time I dropped a shimmering wine-colored long-sleeved top over the dress and created the appearance of a skirt and top set. Thursday, the piece de resistance: I slipped a silver and black lace topper over the dress. It had long sleeves and came down to hip length. Along with my silver evening shoes, I was as well dressed as anyone else at the $2,500-a-plate museum fundraiser. (No, I didn't have to pay for my ticket!)

Friday wrapped things up with a casual outdoor dinner. For that I threw an open weave hand-beaded sweater over my trusty black dress and finished off the trip in absolute style!

Yes, Cinderella returned from every "ball" and

washed her dress before going to bed. Yes, it drip-dried in the tub every day while I was out. But no, no one ever even suspected that I was wearing the same lil' ol' dress over and over. Matter of fact, one writer asked me if I'd brought along my whole closet. I laughed and confessed my one-dress secret.

Where did I get all that stuff? Monday's jacket came from an outlet for $15. Tuesday's jacket was half of a set I picked up at a thrift store for $6.88. Wednesday's dressy top was from a $10 consignment shop pantset. Thursday? That fancy lace topper was a $1.98 thrift store find. And Friday's sweater was a consignment shop buy at $4.

Without even considering the value of the other half of the two outfits part of these items were borrowed from, I don't think $48.86 was a bad investment for all that stuff, do you? I'm telling you, ladies, you don't have to spend even a hundred to look like a million!

Where Do I Start?

Start with what's already in your closet. First, grab a notepad, go through your clothes, and make an inventory. The next step is a toughie: separate sets. Yep, risky though this may be, I want you to break up those jackets and skirts, jackets and pants, jackets and dresses—anything that is a matched set—and begin to look at these items as individual pieces of clothing. Too many of us live in fear of this, never daring to break up a set, never dreaming of putting on one piece without the other.

Another legal clothing move you may have over-looked is putting tops over dresses. It's true. If a vest or jacket can go over a dress, why not a blouse? Try it. Believe it or not, y'all, the clothes police will not come and get you. You won't get arrested; chances are you won't even get a ticket. I'm here to declare freedom! So snatch up those newfound treasures and let's get busy!

Keep writing. As you haul out that yellow and blue plaid jacket, look at the other items on your list and in your closet. Isn't there something else besides that yellow and blue plaid skirt that would work with this piece? Why, yes! Those blue slacks are just the right shade. And wow! That solid blue skirt is a perfect match, too. As you break out of "suit bondage," you're going to find a whole lot of new outfits without ever leaving your closet. Dig on, sister girl—you'll be floored at what you discover.

Can I share one closet example of my own? I rarely wear gray because it's not a good color on me. (If you're familiar with the color-coding system, I'm an autumn.) But I couldn't resist a gorgeous medium gray pair of knit cropped pants on final, final outlet markdown for $1.13. So I brought them home and dug through the closet to see what I could coordinate.

I found a turquoise knit dress with a matching hip-length open jacket (sort of a swing coat style). I'd never before realized that the geometric designs on the lower front of the jacket were done in gray! With a pale gray top added in, the jacket and cropped pants created an adorable outfit and the jacket kept the gray tones from making me looked washed out.

Color Me Cute

It's a fact, girls. Some people look great in colors that other people look not-so-great in, and vice versa. If you want to know your color range (most commonly ranked by seasons: spring, summer, fall, or winter), don't spend a fortune finding out. Head to your local library and check out a book like the now-classic *Color Me Beautiful* or a similar publication. If you're not sure where to begin looking, ask a librarian—these folks know almost everything; and what they don't know, they know how to find out.

Meanwhile, dig through your closet and find all different shades and colors of items that will be worn on your upper body—the key to your best look is keeping the most flattering colors nearest your face. Next, find a well-lighted spot and drape the items across the front of your neck. Keep that pad and pencil handy and note the colors and shades you try and which ones seem to be most becoming. If you're in doubt about this, ask a fashion-minded friend to truthfully help you choose your best colors to work with.

After trying a few garments, you'll begin to see that there are definitely some colors you need to avoid and others that are far more becoming. Note these and commit to memory and to paper the colors that work best for you. (The backside of your occasions list is a good place to make this notation.)

Already you've cut your shopping time by narrowing your looking to a select group of colors. Already you're a *more attractive you* since becoming aware of the colors that most complement your eyes, skin, and hair tone. Already you've found new outfits right inside your very own closet—and without spending a single nickel!

So Now What?

You've scavenged your closet, you've coordinated some new outfits. What next? If you still need to add to your repertoire, plan on buying some basic solid-color pieces as mainstays. A few simple dresses (like my black one) can be worn year-round, dressed up or down, transformed into a skirt/top look, or worn as is.

You'll be amazed—once you've given it a try—how many terrific outfits you can concoct after you have some good basic solids for starters. The next step is finding the right accessories.

Put Your Best Foot Forward

Nothing ruins a pretty outfit quicker than inappropriate, ugly, or cheap-looking shoes. Not to worry. There's a plethora (which is a whole bunch and a really good selection) of marvelous footwear out there awaiting you.

Comfort is my first and foremost priority and should be yours, too. Those ten little toesies and those two little footsies are all you've got and God intends for them to last you a lifetime.

Eliminate the need for so many shoes by choosing styles that hit the middle—in that they're suitable for slacks, skirts, and dresses—and styles that will work all year round. Do you need a shoe to match every single outfit? No. What you need are a few good basic colors such as black, brown, navy, and tan that will coordinate with most anything you choose to put on.

Where to find shoes. Just as with all sorts of other clothing items, I've found incredible buys on shoes in every kind of store from upscale boutiques to yard sales (Some folks refer to these as "tag" sales). And if you're afraid of buying or wearing a used shoe, news flash: get over it. No matter where a shoe comes from, new or used, there's a very good probability your foot isn't the first to have been in it.

Accessory, Accesso-rah!

Nothing puts pizzazz into my plain black dress like a lively set of accessories. I don't mean to repeat myself, but I can't emphasize strongly enough the fact that *everything* is seasonal, including jewelry, scarves, and purses.

At a Chico's outlet sidewalk sale I found an exquisite

necklace made of onyx, turquoise, and other beautiful genuine stones. Regular price? $42. Sale price? 99¢. When I found $40 onyx earrings elsewhere for $15, I couldn't resist. I know, I know. It wasn't 75% off, but I figured the savings on the necklace justified a little bit of splurging.

A colorful scarf can turn the plainest of dresses into a lively outfit. Pins are making a well-deserved comeback. Bracelets are fun to wear. Today's watches are as much fashion as functional. And all can be bought at cut-rate prices when you shop the Bargainomics® way.

Fine jewelry is no exception to the rule. A popular department store chain has a store near me and I love to check out their fine jewelry cases. Always, always, there are at least a handful of pieces that have been drastically reduced.

Where do they hide these? Sometimes in a separate section of the display case, sometimes mixed in. How do I find them? I ask. And their helpful saleslady is eager to show me the very best deals.

Adding or changing accessories can transform an outfit. Be as selective about these as you are about your clothes and you'll be stunning for every occasion.

On the Road Again?

If you do much traveling, I encourage you to look for the new knits that are polyesters, acrylic blends, etc. Like my trusty black dress, these items present few problems with wrinkling or hand-washing. Don't forget that rolling rather than folding guarantees less wrinkles, and if you're unsure of what will travel well, roll the item ahead of time, leave it overnight, and check it the next day.

When I'm out shopping and I'm not sure whether or not a fabric will travel well, I grab a fistful and crush it in my hand. If it goes back to its original condition, it should do okay. If that brief squeeze leaves any wrinkles, it would probably never survive a suitcase.

Now That We're Well-Dressed

Now that we're well dressed on the outside, let's take a little inventory. You know, when the Bible talks about "putting on," it's not referring to airs! What are we to put on? First and foremost, we're to "put on the full armor of God," (Ephesians 6:11), which consists of what? Head-to-toe readiness. If you read that entire passage from Ephesians 6, you'll see the specifics of protective coverings, including our one and only offensive weapon, "the sword of the Spirit, which is the word of God," (Ephesians 6:17).

Girls, if we're to be women of the Word, we've got to know what the Word is, don't we? Better yet, we've got to know who He is: Jesus, "the Word" (John 1:1).

Our first concern shouldn't be what's on the outside. What it should be is what's on the inside. Jesus put it this way in Luke 16:15: "God knows your hearts." He does know our hearts. Is yours focused on Him or on the things of this earth?

There's nothing wrong with working to look our very best, but we should strive to let our outward appearances be extensions of our inner selves. Proverbs 31:25, a section of the familiar "virtuous woman" passage, states that "Strength and dignity are her clothing." As we reflect the beauty of the indwelling Holy Spirit, we also reflect the quiet strength and dignity that we draw from Him.

We who have trusted Jesus Christ as Lord and Savior are the bride of Christ. Our dress, our demeanor, every part of our lives should honor the Bridegroom.

Chapter 6

Let's Start with the Basics— Shelter

"A refuge from the wind and a shelter from the storm."

—Isaiah 32:2

"Mid pleasures and palaces though we may roam, Be it ever so humble, there's no place like home."

—J. H. Payne, *Home, Sweet Home*

If you're expecting in-depth info on renting versus leasing, leasing versus owning, you're not going to find it in this book. What this chapter deals with is home ownership, plain and simple, and how your choice of home matters in the eyes of the Lord.

A Home of Your Own

My father-in-law had a grade school education. He worked long hard hours and he and my mother-in-law raised six children on a meager income. Some years after Larry (their eldest child) and I were married and most of the other kids were also away from home, they managed to put aside enough money to buy their very first home.

I'll never forget the joy on his face when he walked me through that house and showed me every room and cubbyhole. When we got to the last room, he picked me up, swung me around, and grinned like a kid with a brand new toy—I'd never seen this man so elated! After government housing and rental house after rental house, he had become a homeowner.

What about you? Maybe you can't relate to my father-in-law's story, but you still want to know how to find that affordable home of your own. It's out there, you know. And it can be found. And it can be bought. Let me tell you how my own home came about.

Cinderella's Castle

I've been a daddy's girl all my life. I can't remember how old I was the first time my daddy took me fishing, but it was far enough back that I don't recall not ever fishing with him. Those times on the creek bank with our camp stools and minnow bucket were wonderful. I learned to love the country, the outdoors. And that's what I wanted in a home.

As the area we lived in developed more and more, I felt a greater and greater desire to move further away from the big city of Birmingham and out into the peaceful, slower-paced country. I told the Lord the desire of my heart. He said to, didn't He? "Delight yourself in the Lord; and He will give you the desires of your heart" (Psalm 37:4).

"Lord Jesus," I told Him, "what I'd really like to have is a nice ranch-style house and a good-sized garage—separate from the house would be nice. And a few acres of land with it would be good. And what I'd *really* like is for it to be on a quiet, no-traffic street. And if I could be really, really picky, I'd like a little fishing pond, too—you know how I've always loved fishing, dear Father."

Well, guess what? In no time at all I was living in the perfect ranch-style home, right? Nope. In a very short time I was living in a fixer-upper we'd planned to buy and re-sell.

How'd that happen? Blame it on Larry. He decided he

wanted to go ahead and move so that our son Mickey could finish out his high school years in that area. To say I was less than thrilled is an understatement.

"But first," I reminded my husband, "we have to sell our house."

We'd put our house for sale almost a year earlier and then withdrew it when the sellers backed out of the contract for the home we wanted to buy. Days after Larry's decision, the realtor we'd used knocked on our door and asked if we'd still be interested in selling—she had a ready buyer offering a very nice price for our house. So much for reminding Larry we needed to sell first.

So off we moved to the preferred school district. Our new house had steep narrow stairs to a basement laundry facility; it was on a road that was a main thoroughfare for truck traffic between the main highway and a power plant. We had painted, carpeted, wallpapered, and more, and the place looked really nice; but it sure wasn't a ranch-style, and it had no garage at all. What had happened?

Had I mis-prayed? Had the Lord mis-heard? No. I believed in my heart that the Lord would give me that desire of my heart (or change that desire), so I continued to wait patiently (more or less!) on His timing.

A year or so after we'd moved, I was driving in our area and spotted a real estate sign pointing down a narrow paved road. Turning in, I saw that there were only three houses on the entire street. Each house was surrounded by several acres of property, and at the end of the road was an enormous lake, complete with a tiny log cabin on the shoreline. I was ecstatic!

Just before the lake on the right side of the street, a long gravel drive led to a ranch-style house with a roomy garage peeking out from behind. "Lord, my house!" I shouted inside my car. Hurrying home, I called the realtor.

The lake didn't belong to that house, but a smaller pond behind the garage was included. There were six gently rolling acres, and grand old oak and hickory trees graced the front lawn. It was perfect—until she told me the asking price.

Hard as it was to swallow, the house was completely out of our league. "Okay, Lord," I choked out, "I still don't believe You showed me that house for nothing. It's exactly what I want. If that isn't my house, then I still thank You for showing it to me because now I know that we're both on the same wavelength (as if He could goof up!); You know just what I want and I'm trusting You to provide it in Your time."

Another year later, my friend Sherry and I were relaxing after church. As I did my usual read through the real estate ads in Sunday's paper, I jumped from my chair and shouted "Hallelujah!" (No small thing for a Southern Baptist).

There it was in black and white: a foreclosure notice for a home with acreage and a pond. How did I know it was that very house? All I can tell you is that I knew. I yanked Sherry from her nest on the loveseat and we piled into the car and drove over.

In the front window of the den was the most beautiful sign I'd ever read in my life: *Foreclosure Notice*. The sign listed the name and contact number for a Birmingham realtor. We walked around, peering in every window (the house was vacant). Already my head was swimming with ideas on how to fix this and change that. Sherry later told me that she—not for the first time—was questioning my sanity.

When the realtor answered my call, I was fervently praying for the price to be substantially lower than it had been when I'd looked at it before. Imagine my astonishment when I was quoted *one-half* of the original asking price.

"I want this house," I heard myself blurting into the phone. "I want your verbal commitment right now that I'm your buyer." And the man agreed and arranged a time to meet me at the property. Sherry went with me to the appointment.

Sherry, like many people I know, can't see what's not right there in front of her. While I saw a wonderful, roomy house, she saw a money pit of old carpet, ugly wallpaper, and disrepair. Now (we've bought several fixer-uppers over the years) she no longer doubts my ability to get the uglies out of most any house.

Secondly, Larry is a true helpmate sent from God. He wasn't even particularly surprised when I came home and told him I'd agreed to buy that house. Now ladies, I don't recommend you try house-buying without your spouse's approval, but this was one occasion when I knew that I knew that I knew that *that house* was for us.

Amazingly, as we prepared to sign our names along the dotted lines, we both felt impressed to make an offer. *Make an offer?* I remember thinking. *This thing is already cheaper than we could ever have dreamed or imagined!*

But the impression was so strong that we did it. We offered less money. And they took it. Several more years and several thousand dollars later, the house appraised for *four times* what we'd originally agreed to pay.

Where do you begin? As I've said in a million other places, start with prayer. Tell the Lord what you want and then ask Him to give you what He wants you to have. If you are truly seeking Him, either He will give you that desire or He will change that desire to conform to what He knows is best.

Waiting on the Lord. If you look back over my house story, you'll see that God doesn't always move at lightning speed. He can, but thankfully He usually doesn't. When I think of what a disaster it would have been to end up in the house we'd originally tried to buy, I am so grateful that the Lord rescued us from our foolishness. He had a plan for us and He has a plan for you.

What's the difference between "killing time" and "waiting on the Lord?" Contentment. Peace. Confidence. Contentment that God is patiently working for your good. Peace that He knows what is best for you. Confidence, not in and of ourselves, but confidence in Him ("O Lord God, You are my confidence." Psalm 71:5) to do for you the best thing at the best time.

So What's Right for Me?

You're the only one who can answer that question. You're the only one who can attune your heart to God's and know His will for you. The most important thing to remember is that when God opens a door, He fully opens it.

There's a contemporary song that says, "When God closes a door, He opens a window," but even though I love the song and most of its sentiment, I don't really agree with the window. You see, when God opens something, you don't have to squeeze your way in. A window might be a pretty tight squeeze; a cracked door has to be pried open.

A door opened by the Lord swings wide. Whether you're trying to buy a house, change jobs, or make any other decision, you can take it to the bank: You will never have to force yourself through a door that the Lord has opened.

Yes, I put a lot of stipulations on what I wanted. But

what I didn't do is put a lot on what I would accept. I had asked for a quiet street. I didn't get it—at first. I had asked for a garage. I didn't get one—at first.

What He did give me was time. Time to learn to trust Him more. Time so that, when at last He led me to my "castle," I could look beyond the mildew, bad tile, and broken windows, and be totally in awe of His gracious provision.

The ugliest house on the street. Read anything you want to pick up about investing in real estate and it'll tell you to buy the cheapest house in the neighborhood. Choosing a good area far outweighs choosing a pretty house. As long as a home is structurally sound, cosmetics are nothin'—you ought to see me when I wake up in the morning!

Next, check with local authorities. The school board can answer all your questions about local schools, including their scholastic standings and more. The local police can provide crime statistics that will help you determine the general safety of the community. As a responsible steward, all these avenues are open to you and should be taken advantage of.

Make a list. You can tell by now that I'm really big on lists. Sit down and write out a list of everything you want in a home. Dream big. List everything. Next, make another list of what you could realistically live with. Now, beside the "dream list," number the items in order of priority. If a jacuzzi is your biggest wish, then mark a "1" out beside it. If it's a fireplace, mark that. Go through the whole list and rank all your wants.

Get specific. If you went to look for a car, would you pull into the first dealership you happened to pass? No. You'd find out where one was for the type of car you had in mind and then go to it, wouldn't you? Likewise, get specific when you pray.

Tell the Lord as I did. "Lord, what I want is . . ." But when you finish asking for that want, tell Him *from your heart* that what you want most is whatever He wants you to have.

After I asked the Lord for my ranch-style house, garage, land, and pond, I also admitted to the Lord that He knew far better than I what we really needed and that I trusted Him to direct us to whatever place He wanted us to live. You can't fake sincerity, ladies. Can you honestly tell God that accepting His leading is a greater desire of your heart than getting what you think you want?

Start shopping. Mr. Pious was hungry and he began to pray for food. "O Lord," he pleaded. "I'm down to nothing. My cupboard is bare. Send your provision as I wait for your great hand of mercy." The man sat down in the middle of the floor and waited. After a time the phone began to ring.

"No," Mr. Pious declared, "I'll not budge from this spot until the Lord has answered my prayer." Eventually the phone stopped its chirping.

"Oh, I do wish Mr. Pious was home," Miss Helpsgift told herself as she put down her receiver. "I so wanted to take him this casserole."

A little later the doorbell rang. Weaker now, the man could only whisper, "I'll not be hindered from waiting on the Lord."

Outside Miss Helpsgift pressed the button one more time. "Oh, I do wish he was home, but I'll just leave this dish on the porch. Surely he won't be away long." Miss Helpsgift departed and the doorbell was once again silent.

Did the Lord rain down manna from heaven and feed this hungry man? He could have, no doubt about it. But what the Lord had already done was send someone to minister to his needs. Right outside his door was the very thing Mr. Pious had prayed for. But the man had refused to even budge.

Are you beginning to see the light? We can't sit and wait on our manna from heaven, even if we believe with all our hearts that God is 100% capable of delivering to us in that manner. What He expects us to do is to actively seek His will and His way.

Use every resource you can find to check into foreclosures, lease/purchases, loan programs, and other information that can help you achieve the desire of your heart. "Pray without ceasing" (1 Thessalonians 5:17) as you contact lending institutions, scour the libraries, read books, and scout out real estate ads and booklets.

When King David told his people that he would go out and help the army to fight, the people protested, saying, "it is better that you be ready to help" (2 Samuel 18:3). Likewise, as David accepted the counsel of his people and did not go, we need to both seek and listen to the advice and counsel of our godly peers, and we also need to be cautious not to leap first and pray later.

Don't expect to scan a couple of websites and then be prepared to make the single greatest buy in all of real estate history. Don't expect the home of your dreams to fall from the sky into your lap as you sit idle and pray for it to happen. And don't sign a contract for a house and then ask the Lord to bless your decision. Ask God first. What did Jesus tell us in Matthew 6:33? "But seek first His kingdom and His righteousness, and all these things will be added to you." Don't insult the Lord by including Him as an afterthought. Let Him be the beginning and continuing focus of your request.

Proverbs 24:27 speaks of keeping things in the right order. (See also Proverbs 27:23–26.) It tells us what things are to be done first to prepare and goes on to say: "Afterwards, then, build your house." There has to be a *before* in order for there to an *after*, right?

Pray. Do your homework (research, research, research), then pray some more. And when all that preparation is complete, wait on the Lord's timing. When He directs you to a house, you won't have to force the transaction into fruition. He will swing the door completely open.

Chapter 7

Making a House a Home

"When Jesus came into Peter's home . . . his mother-in-law . . . got up and waited on Him."
—**Matthew 8:14–15**

"Ah, what is more blessed than to put cares away, when the mind lays by its burden, and tired with labour of far travel we have come to our own home and rest on the couch we have longed for? This it is which alone is worth all these toils."
—**The writings of Catullus, c. 84–54** B.C.

W hether you share space with a roommate, own, rent, or lease, your space is still your castle. Like mine, it may not be a million-dollar mansion, but it's what you call home. You want your living quarters to look great and be distinctively yours.

Whether you're in the thinking stages or in the middle of refurnishing and redecorating, this chapter has plenty for you to think about. Philippians 4:19 declares that "my God will supply all your needs according to His riches in glory in Christ Jesus." If you have a need for furnishings and decoration, your answer is only a prayer (and perhaps a bit of elbow grease) away!

Before we go there, I want to give you some spectacular food for thought from Max Lucado's *Traveling Light for Mothers*. Using the 23rd Psalm as the basis for this section of the book, Lucado says: "It's as if [David] is saying, 'What I have in God is greater than what I don't have in life.'"

Maybe you can't afford a $20,000 sofa, but what you really can't afford is to be discontent with what the Lord has provided for you. Jesus Christ is sufficient. Approach everything you do, including furnishing and decorating your home, from this all-important mindset.

Let me reiterate about using your income wisely. Hopefully a tithe and offerings are already regular parts of the checks you write each month, but if they're not, let me urge you to do what we just read in the previous chapter:

"seek first." Give God the firstfruits of all you receive and He will abundantly bless your obedience. You'll find that what you have left after your tithes and offerings will do more than what the entire amount would have had done had you neglected to tithe.

God is completely faithful. He will return to you that which you entrust to Him—and more. Jesus explained this fact in Luke 6:38: "Give, and it will be given to you . . . a good measure—pressed down, shaken together, and running over. For by your standard of measure, it will be measured to you in return."

Whether it was money or service, whatever I have done in servanthood to the Lord, I have received manyfold in return. He stands ready and able to do the same for you.

First Furnishings

The first thing we want to furnish our homes with is prayer. Psalm 127:1 warns: "Unless the Lord builds the house, they labor in vain." Unless the Lord is first place in your heart, unless He is the center of your life, the most expensive, elegantly furnished home on the planet will never satisfy that emptiness inside you.

You are God's spiritual house on this earth, child of God. ("Your body is a temple of the Holy Spirit who is in you" 1 Corinthians 6:19.) Therefore anywhere you are, including your home, is His dwelling place. Make certain that everything within and without your home welcomes His presence.

The Big Stuff

Appliances. These things can cost a fortune! If you're set on new ones, prepare to spend a bundle; but with careful shopping, you can find the very best prices on the items you have in mind. Several stores offer a guarantee that they will meet or beat any other store's prices. Some also promise that if you can buy from them and then find the item elsewhere for less (within a specified period of time, along with other stipulations), they'll refund you the difference plus a little extra for your trouble.

Let your fingers do the walking. Phone stores and look online for the best deals before wandering around the universe. And when you visit an appliance store, take along the exact measurements for the spaces these appliances will have to fit.

Be ready to ask: (1) What's the warranty on this appliance? (2) Exactly what's included? For example, an electric stove is sometimes sold without the "pigtail," which is the cord that plugs into the electrical outlet. Refrigerators are often displayed with icemakers that must be added in at an additional charge.

Other questions to ask: (3) Will you sell the display model for less? (4) Do any of these currently offer rebates? (5) Do you discount for cash? (6) What about delivery? Is there a charge? If so, how much? (7) And if installation of any kind is necessary, how much do you charge for that?

It all boils down to being an informed consumer. And the best informer is the Lord. Ask Him to accompany you and lead you as you shop for everything you plan to put in your home.

I've heard some people say, "I'm just trusting the Lord to take care of my needs." Let me ask you this: If I buy a Bible, sleep with it under my pillow every night, and ask the Lord to fill me with its wisdom, will He do it? He's capable, yes. But He expects me to do my part—if I want to know God's Word, I'll have to read it. And if I want to be a smart consumer, I'll have to study up on the products I want to go out and buy.

Used appliances can be purchased from individuals, from used appliance places, and from thrift stores such as the Salvation Army and Goodwill. Individuals generally offer the lowest prices, but not always. What individuals don't offer that many second-hand and thrift shops do is a warranty. Most of the large and small appliances I've purchased at thrift stores carry a 30-day warranty. But ask, to be certain; don't take any of this for granted.

Another thing to consider before buying from an individual or most thrift stores is delivery. Unless you have the means to get the appliance home unassisted (or are with friends who won't charge you for their help), make sure you add in the cost of delivery before deciding which place has the best buy.

Avoid buying a used appliance that isn't shown to be operational. I realize this isn't always possible, but wherever it can be done, insist on a demonstration.

Furniture. With the change of seasons comes change in furniture stores. Out with the old patterns, in with the new—and out you can go with a wonderful buy. Shop retail stores, factory directs, other outlet-type places, and salvage stores.

Take along room measurements. That oversized sofa may look grand on the showroom floor, but it won't be nearly so lovely sticking out six inches into your doorway! You might even want to sketch a rough layout of each of your rooms (including window heights and locations) and bring that as well.

If you're replacing furniture, measure the old stuff, even if you're going for a completely different look. At least by comparing the size, you'll have an idea of how the new things will look in your home. Those 28-inch square end tables may look great in that showroom, but it'll take one heavyweight sofa to balance the effect of their size.

Make sure you look past the glitz of the display and look at the item itself. Don't rush. Sit on sofas, lie down on mattresses (no matter how goofy you feel—I do recommend you wear pants when you try this!), sit on chairs, open and close drawers and doors.

Particularly if you'll be buying the very item you're

looking at, check it from one end to the other for nicks, tears, and other defects. If you find a small problem you can live with, use it as bargaining leverage and insist on a discount.

Once you've located that affordable and workable piece of furniture, start asking questions:

(1) What's the warranty on this?

(2) Exactly what's included? Are these throw pillows included or are they strictly for display? Especially in a salvage or outlet store, make sure any unattached part is available and included.

(3) Will you make me a better price on the one on display?

(4) Do any of these currently offer rebates? (Yes, rebates are sometimes offered on furnishings.)

(5) Do you discount for cash?

(6) What about delivery? Is there a charge? If so, how much?

(7) Is assembly of any kind necessary? How much do you charge for that?

I love used furnishings. From the antique to the fun and funky, some people seem to never tire of changing decor—and wise stewards love to go after these bargains. Much of the information above can also be applied whenever you're shopping for used furniture.

But when dealing with used pieces, you can let your imagination go wild! *(What would that piece look like if I painted it orange?)* Used furniture is like an ugly house. Is it structurally sound? 'Cause if it is, we can work the uglies right on outa that thing!

In my bedroom there's an oak chifforobe (an armoire with drawers) that I bought for $15 at a thrift store. The mirrors were broken and cardboard had been stapled on to cover the openings. The knobs were missing. But I saw beyond all this. With a little help from my dad, we stripped off the old finish, re-stained and tung-oiled the whole thing, put in new mirrors, and added new knobs. Total investment (excluding sweat and tears): $28.

I found a dresser with no mirror and a 4-drawer chest for $10 at a yard sale. Sure, they were olive green, but they were well worth the price after they were transformed with the help of some hard work. At a thrift store I located a mirror frame that fit the dresser exactly ($2.98) and at another one I found the right-sized mirror ($1.98). At a flea market, I located a little wooden stool, the perfect complement to this '40s-style dresser ($14).

Along with a yard sale chair ($10); a pair of glass-topped metal night stands ($20); and a king-size metal bed from an outlet store ($135), I have furnished my master bedroom for a grand total of $221.96. Not bad.

Decorating

Girls, you don't have to spend a fortune to have a charming, comfortably furnished home. Once you learn to use a few simple principles, you'll find you can have beautiful things without paying the marked-up price. Even if you're not crafty yourself, you probably know someone who can help you. Here are some basics.

Sew what? I hear you: you don't sew. Neither do I. But in that mysterious corner at WalMart and other stores with a fabric or crafts section, you'll find all sorts of neat products for us sewless sisters. When it comes to decorating with fabric, these goodies make it as easy as pie.

Annie, get your gun. A glue gun is my tool of choice. The base model sells for less than $2 and a whopping bag of glue sticks costs about the same. Then there's fabric glue—also terrific stuff. Without a pattern or, in my case, any skill whatsoever, it's possible to create elegant home decor of every kind.

I always pick up inexpensive fabrics from the clearance stacks since (a) I'm cheap; and (b) I have yet to develop great confidence in what might turn out. But often, with a little gluing and folding, I manage to concoct some fairly impressive decorations.

Oftentimes I use an iron to hurry-dry and press fabric-glued seams into place. Whenever I do this, I put a piece of thin cotton fabric (like cheesecloth) between the iron and the glued fabric to keep glue from adhering to my iron.

A window of opportunity. What have I made? My best creation has been my curtain rods. First I measured my windows and determined how long these would need to be. Then I went to a home improvement store and had sections of 2 1/2" diameter PVC pipe (the white plastic stuff used for plumbing) cut according to my measurements—they didn't even charge extra for cutting it.

Next, I went to a rug and drapery outlet and picked up really elegant-looking ceramic rod holders for $8 each. After that, I hit the clearance fabric stack and purchased several yards of $1-a-yard fabric and a package of 4" styrofoam balls (to be used as finials).

Step by step, here's how to make the window dressings:

1. Cut the fabric to fit around the piece of pipe, leaving 2" excess on each end of the pipe.

2. Use a glue gun to glue the fabric smoothly around the pipe; then trim any excess at the "seam" (to be turned toward the wall).

3. Tuck the excess fabric at the ends into the pipe and glue it in place.

4. Cut pieces of fabric big enough to completely and neatly wrap around a styrofoam ball while leaving enough excess to use a twist tie to securely tie the fabric into place. (It takes two balls for each window—one for each end of the pipe.)

5. Use the glue gun to dot glue around the twist tie to ensure it will not come undone.

6. Trim the excess fabric so that only a small "poof" extends from one side of the ball.

7. Encircle the edge of the inside of one end of the pipe with hot glue and then quickly insert the "poof" end of a fabric-wrapped ball. (This completes one end of your new curtain rod.)

8. Install a rod holder on each side of the window.

9. Slide the open end of the rod into the holder and glue the other ball in place on the open end of the rod.

Once all that was done, I took more fabric and made a window scarf, folding, gluing, and ironing the hems into place. I draped the scarf around the rod and ended up with one elegantly frocked little window!

Note: If you want to hang drapes/curtains on the rod, install the rod somewhat differently:

(a) Install the rod holders so that they can be removed again while leaving their mounting screws in place.

(b) Slide one rod holder onto the rod/pipe and push it over to the end that already has a ball attached.

(c) Slide the drapes/curtains onto the rod.

(d) Slide the other rod holder onto the rod.

(e) Glue the second fabric-wrapped ball into place on the open end of the rod.

(f) Fit the rod holders back onto their mounting screws. Voila! Your entire window treatment will now be in place.

Wall to wall. Some of my favorite wall decorations are framed photos; but I'm not talking about the family portrait gallery. Instead of spending a lot of money for a picture you're going to find in plenty of other houses, or instead of paying for an inexpensive painting that looks it, why not mat and frame enlargements of your own photography?

A favorite shrub in full bloom. A blow-up of a scene from your parents' or grandparents' childhood. When it comes to your own shots, don't worry about not being a professional—anything that meant enough for you to hang onto is nice enough to grace the walls of your home.

Umpteen (which is a whole lot) different stores offer photo services, including enlargements, at very reasonable prices. For smaller spaces, you'll be totally impressed with what you can do with a framed and matted 3x5 or 4x6 standard ol' snapshot. Larger spots can be complemented with 5x7, 8x10, and 11x14 enlargements—no matter what quality the photograph, framing and matting can make all the difference.

Frames can be fairly expensive—in some cases, unbelievably so. A good starting point for frame shopping is your local thrift store or a yard sale. The trick is to look at the frame and not what's in it. Forget the fact that there's a giant paint-by-numbers clown in that frame! Is the frame itself in good condition? Will a little Old English Scratch Cover take care of any problems? Can it be refinished? How about painting it? Is the glass in good condition? If the price, frame, and glass are acceptable, buy it. Any mats that are included are a bonus.

What about mats? New, these can cost anywhere from a dollar to ten dollars, depending on the size and whether it's a single or double (one layered over another). Familiarize yourself with the general pricing of these and be ready to grab any bargain frames or pictures that include a really nice mat.

There's simply no comparison between a plain framed photo and one with a pretty mat. And once you've started creating your own wall hangings, you'll want to do some extra ones as gifts.

More Decor

Read all about it. If you can't envision what you want a room to look like, scan decorating, remodeling, and home magazines to come up with ideas. Hit the thrift store or, if your library has a bookstore, check it out; both of these places—and yard sales, too—are excellent sources of magazines. These places offer plenty of current or at least recent publications, so why pay newsstand prices? For the normal cost of one, you can take home a bagful.

eBay away. There are many online auctions, but eBay (www.ebay.com) is definitely the largest. I've bought gorgeous oil paintings, frames, sculptures, table napkins, and more, and out of dozens and dozens of transactions, have had no real problems. (One framed poster arrived with the glass broken, but the package was insured and I was reimbursed.)

The great estate. Classified ads in newspapers frequently include notices for probate court and private estate sales/auctions. The word *estate* may make it sound grand, but this isn't necessarily so. While it could actually be the home, cars, and land of what we think of as a truly grand estate, it could also be the contents of a small apartment. "Estate" simply refers to an individual's possessions.

In general, a probate court's sale of property will be done by auction, with an actual auctioneer offering from a numbered list either individually or in groupings or "lots" every item that is to be sold. (Each piece is tagged with an individual or lot number.) Since antique and second-hand dealers frequent these events, expect heavy bidding on true antiques and collectibles.

When planning to attend an auction, attend the preview day if one is offered. Many times, items can be viewed a day or two ahead of time. All at least offer a few hours of preview opportunity prior to the auction's start time. This allows prospective bidders to pick up a list of items to be auctioned, look around, and note items they want.

If you have the time and patience to stick around, the crowd thins as the number of items diminishes; and when time becomes pressing, items are sold at a faster pace with less time for bid prices to climb skyward. Too, items are sometimes grouped together in order to move things along at a faster pace. Here's when the best buys are available.

When it comes to private estate sales, these can be done by auction, same as probate court, or items may already be priced. In some cases, prices are firm; in others, there's room for negotiation. How do you know which is which? Make an offer! The worst thing they can tell you is no! (Digging through a box of books labeled "$1 each," I discovered a very nice 1888 edition of *Pilgrim's Progress*. No, I did not negotiate on the price!)

Depending on the rules of the sale or auction (if these aren't posted, ask) be prepared to either take your items with you or return at a later date to pick them up. Know what forms of payment are acceptable: some insist on cash only; others will accept personal checks, debit cards, and credit cards. Make sure any items to be picked up are clearly tagged with your name or bidding number and that your payment receipt indicates that this merchandise is to be picked up at another time.

Other auctions. Businesses, cities, colleges, and even government departments have auctions. In many of these cases, no advertising is done via newspaper. Your best bet is to make direct contact with these places and ask about the possibility of auctions.

For example, the hospital where I was employed auctions surplus merchandise at least once or twice every year. My first solid wood office desk came from there for only $16. From medical equipment to conference and waiting room furnishings, there are plenty of goodies that would work well for home use.

Many police departments auction "seized" property, merchandise confiscated during an arrest. Items that remain unclaimed by their legal owners will most likely end up in one of these. What can you expect to find? Virtually anything—from junk to jewelry, televisions to toasters. Whatever got nabbed will turn up here, giving you the chance to grab a bargain.

Chapter 8

Gifts

"Their father gave them many gifts of silver, gold and precious things."

—2 Chronicles 21:3

"Do not trust the horse, Trojans! Whatever it is, I fear the Greeks even when they bring gifts."

—Virgil, *The Aeneid*

If you're one to skip around when reading a book, now would be a good time to flip back and read the chapter on shopping. It includes information about the all-important occasions list for gift giving.

The Card-inal Sin

Okay, maybe it's not a *sin*, but it's at least something to seriously think about. If you're going to send a card, let that suffice. If you're going to buy a gift, save your card money. For the price of many cards you can give a very nice gift instead—and call me crazy, but I prefer gifts to cards!

"E" Me

Cards are what I send when I want to acknowledge someone's birthday without sending a gift. With postage prices going ever higher, I use Internet e-cards whenever possible. Websites like Hallmark's (www.hallmark.com) and Dayspring's (www.dayspring.com) are among hundreds that offer free e-mail greeting cards. You can choose the card you want to send, add your own sentiment (some even let you choose music, backgrounds, and more), and schedule it to be sent on the appropriate date. If you have friends with e-mail, what better way to send along a greeting? And these free e-cards aren't just for birthdays, either. Like paper cards, these can be found for every occasion from "Just to Say Hello" to "Happy Groundhog Day."

What's the catch? What's the gimmick? Why are these free? Simple. As with most everything on the Internet (and television and newspapers and magazines), these sites carry advertising as well as other merchandise that isn't free. And it's their fondest hope that, while you are picking out your freebie e-cards, you'll also take an interest in one of their not-free products or services.

Revive 'Em Again

When you give a gift, especially if you're attending a tea, shower, or party where a number of other gifts will also be present, you want some sort of card on your package. This is where recycling comes in. Any time I receive a card, I save it and use it to make my own gift cards or tags.

From the envelope to the front, back, and inside, I re-use every workable part of the cards I receive. If a card has a beautiful rainbow across the front, I cut out the rainbow and write the "To" and "From" across it. If there's a meaningful verse inside, I cut around it and use it as my gift card. When even the tiniest gift cards average around $1 apiece, why not forgo that expense and put that money into the gift instead? With a little practice, the price of that card can buy your gift!

Make Your Own

Besides cutting up old cards, you can also buy special card paper or card stock that can be used to create your own cards on your computer. If you'll take the time to check out all the programs you already have, there's a good chance one of these will create greeting cards.

If not, these programs can be bought for little money and will allow you to create a variety of designs and styles. If a graduation, wedding, tea, or other occasion is in your future, this might be a very good investment. Matching envelopes (in proper sizes and colors) can be bought inexpensively in office supply departments or stores and at party goods suppliers. You can also buy sheets of blank business cards to run on your computer. Use these to create spectacular personalized gift cards to use for every occasion.

Basket Cases

One of the prettiest ways to put several smaller gift items together is to place them in a basket. Baskets of all shapes and sizes can be bought for little or nothing in stores, at yard sales, and at thrift shops.

To clean a used basket, spread an old towel that you don't mind getting stained onto your kitchen countertop. Fill one side of your sink 2/3 full of water and add in 1 cup of bleach. Dip each basket, then place it on the towel to dry. Your used baskets will then be clean and ready to use!

After Easter is always a great time to pick up new baskets, "grass," and cellophane at 75% off or better. But even without the grass filler or cellophane, you can still put together a great-looking gift basket. Got a paper shredder or know someone who does? Shred the Sunday comic section to create colorful basket filler. Any plastic wrap in your kitchen? Use this to wrap your basket—it'll stick well in most places and tiny bits of tape can be used wherever a little help is needed.

Tin to Agree

Tins aren't only for fruitcakes any more. Especially around Christmastime, stores carry tins packed with T-shirts, hankies, golf balls, golf tees, and all sorts of other stuff. Why pay the store when you can pack your own gift the same way?

Tins can be rounded up just like baskets—in regular stores, at yard sales, and at thrift shops. A good washing with soap and water is all these really need. Fill them with Easter grass or shredded paper and arrange your gift items inside.

Get Potted

If you know someone enjoys plants, a flowerpot can be used as a gift container in the same way as a basket or tin. Dollar stores often carry an excellent variety of decorative flowerpots. Yard sales and thrift shops are always good sources, too.

If you do know someone who'd enjoy a plant as a gift, instead of spending a fortune for a beautifully potted plant, buy one in a plain plastic container. Then transfer it to your pretty bargain pot before you present it.

Spinning a Yarn

The absolute best ribbon you'll ever discover is yarn. One skein can wrap a gazillion packages. Double, triple, or quadruple the strands to form a good ribbon, then do the same to tie a nice bow. The more you work with yarn, the more ideas you'll come up with.

Use yarn to tie off the top of your basket's cellophane or plastic wrap, and cover your tie with a fluffy yarn bow. Mixing different colors of yarn together allows you to create fabulous complements to your gift packaging.

Coolest of all, as you wrap and stack packages, there's no more hassle with situating items so that the bows don't get crushed. If you flatten out the yarn, a bit of hand-fluffing will bring it back out good as new.

It's a Wrap

Butcher paper or rolled paper (for instance, rolls of disposable tablecloth paper) makes super year-round giftwrap. Add stickers and the ever-lovely yarn ribbon and bow to dress up the packaging.

• After Christmas, look for solid-colored gift-wrap and patterns that can be used for other occasions. Prices (naturally) should be down to 75% off before you buy, but this will enable you to not only stock up on plenty of paper to use throughout the year, but also to load up for next year's Christmas wrapping.

• Don't toss those old maps, either. These make the perfect gift wrap for those who love to travel, are heading off to college, moving, or taking that special vacation.

• Check thrift stores, yard sales, bargain bins, and around your own home for leftover wallpaper. This works perfectly as gift-wrap (and as shelf paper, too).

• Newspaper can be transformed into adorable packaging when topped with a cute yarn ribbon and bow. Sunday comics are perfect packaging, too. Got a Garfield fan among your friends and family? How about Peanuts? These pages are not only festive—they're free!

• Ordinary brown paper bags can be cut open and used as gift-wrap. You'll be amazed how a bit of colorful ribbon and bow dresses it up. Bag gifts in these, too, and hot glue on a yarn bow as a finishing touch.

Free and Almost-Free Goodies

Samples. A while back I received a sample pack of flavored instant coffees through the mail—two little envelopes of one serving each. Since I'm not a huge fan of coffee (and Larry thinks anything besides plain ol' coffee isn't manly), I tucked these away in my gift closet.

Some time later a friend was down with the flu and I wanted to take her a little get-well package. I'd found a set of 4 stoneware mugs on clearance for only a dollar, so I took one of those, stuffed it with a bit of Easter grass, tucked in the coffee samples, wrapped it in plastic wrap, and topped it with a yarn bow. It wasn't a lot, but it was certainly a day-brightener for Gwendolyn.

Hotel goodies. No, not the towels and ashtrays. But any time I travel I save the unused soaps, lotions, coffees, etc. from my hotel rooms. These can be assembled into great little gift packets. It's not how much you spend that puts a smile on the face of a true friend—it's simply the fact that you were thinking of her.

Give yourself. Homemade gift certificates are wonderful. My sister-in-law Kathy is a saint. She knows how much I despise ironing, so she gave me the gift of one hour of ironing for my birthday. Nothing else she could have done would have been more thoughtful.

Especially for those living alone, there is no greater gift than the gift of time. For the elderly, instead of giving her her 15th container of dusting powder, why not offer her two hours of yard work or deliver a meal and then stay and enjoy it along with her?

A dollar'll do. As I said in the shopping chapter, dollar stores (where every item is a dollar) can hold some amazing bargains. From name-brand products to best-selling authors, a visit to one of these may net you some terrific gift items. What have I bought as gifts? At least a dozen Christian books, countless children's Bible story-books, awesome CDs, a couple of great movies, some name-brand jewelry items, way-cool sunglasses, and tons of wonderfully fragrant bath products.

Other Ideas

Gift cards and certificates. Can't come up with a gift idea? Why not a gift card or certificate? These are available for virtually everything: restaurants, grocers, oil changes, home improvement stores, bookstores, pest control, manicures, hairdressers, and more. Think outside the traditional. An oil change may not sound very personal, but considering the out-of-pocket expense it will save, it might be exactly the thing that is needed.

Phone cards. For anyone with friends or relatives at a distance, a phone card makes a welcome and useful gift. Be selective, though, and know what you're buying. Prices vary widely and so do other restrictions.

Think out of season. If Aunt Susie's birthday is January but her favorite hobby is gardening, what's wrong with giving her a set of gardening tools? Or how about a piece of outdoor statuary?

Two of my sisters-in-law, Kathy and Karen, love the beach. Once a year they have a yard sale and use the money for their annual "ladies only" getaway. The husbands keep the kids and the moms head to the sand 'n' sea. At Christmas I presented them with beach bags, sandals, and sunglasses—and they loved them.

Feed me! Food is a great gift, but make sure you're

aware of any diet restrictions or allergies. I can't get over the prices charged for premixed jars of ingredients for brownies, soups, etc. Good grief, y'all! Can't we even figure out how to fill up a jar anymore?

Layer your ingredients in a nice clean canning type jar, top the lid with a decorative cover (Use yarn to tie a circle of fabric or gift wrap around it.), and tie on (to the same piece of yarn) a card with preparation instructions. If any perishable items are needed to complete the recipe, don't include them, but be sure to note them on the card.

Picture this. Remember those photos we were enlarging, framing, and matting for our own homes? Well, these make fantastic gifts, too. And not only photos work well for this—so do calendars. My last year's Scripture calendar has become a dozen gorgeous framed prints for gift-giving. Find the right size frame or cut the picture and verse to fit what you already have on hand.

The Greatest Gift

What's the greatest gift you've ever been given? I hope your answer is a resounding *"Jesus!"* Jesus told the Samaritan woman, "If you knew the gift of God . . . He would have given you living water" (John 4:10).

The woman at the well wanted such a gift. She wanted to know about this gift of God. Jesus left no doubt when He said: "I who speak to you am He" (v. 26).

Have you experienced the greatest gift of all? Have

you accepted Jesus Christ as Lord and Savior of your life? If you have, are you sharing this Gift with others?

No matter how much money you spend, a material gift is still only a temporary possession. Jesus is forever. He is the gift of life. He is the Living Water. Make sure He's the first gift you share with your loved ones.

Chapter 9

And We're Off! Travel

"Entering the house of Philip the evangelist . . . we stayed with him."

—Acts 21:8

"I must down to the seas again,
To the lonely sea and the sky,
And all I ask is a tall ship and a star to steer her by,
And the wheel's kick and the wind's song
And the white sail's shaking,
And a grey mist on the sea's face
And grey dawn breaking."

—John Masefield, *Sea Fever*

Vacation! What a wonderful word, and what a wonderful opportunity to get away from the norm and enjoy a time of quiet, a family gathering, or an exhilarating once-in-a-lifetime adventure. Wherever you're headed, unless you have friends or relatives to stay with, you're going to need a reasonable, quality place to rest your weary head.

Reserve, Reserve, Cancel

That phrase: "Reserve, reserve, cancel," needs to be etched in your memory as you begin your search for bargain accommodations. What does it mean? Particularly if you're going to need a room during an area's busiest season or during a special event or convention, you'll want to go ahead and lock down something as soon as possible. When you find an available room at a price you can live with, go ahead: reserve.

Whether it's a busy time or not, you want to make a reservation, true? But let's say after you reserve a room at Hotel A, you discover another accommodation with more amenities or a lower rate, or both. What do you do? Reserve. Make that second reservation.

So okay, you've reserved a room, found a better deal, and reserved it. Now what? Cancel. Call the place you first reserved and cancel that reservation. Now you're all set.

But what if before you leave on your trip you find an even better deal somewhere else? No problem. Repeat the same process. Make the second reservation, then call and cancel the other one.

The critical thing is to make certain that you keep a record of your confirmation number (the number they assign you when you make your reservation) and your cancellation number (which is assigned once you cancel). If you are not assigned numbers for either or both of these transactions, make sure you write down the name of the employee(s) with whom you spoke on both occasions. (Even if you are assigned numbers, it's always a good idea to write down the names of the people you talk with.)

Also be aware of specific accommodations' cancellation policies—you'll want to ask about this before even making a reservation. Typically, there's no penalty as long as you cancel at least 72 hours in advance, but don't take my word for it—ask.

Find Those Discounts

It's a date! Very few accommodations maintain a one-price year-round rate. (The most probable exception to this would be a bed & breakfast.) Generally, a set low, mid, and peak season calendar is used, with rates climbing highest during peak season. If you have any flexibility in scheduling your time away from home, try to match your stay to low season.

Who wants to vacation on the beach in the icy throes of winter? Personally, I love a January or February walk on the beach. Nippy, yes, but definitely not crowded! Or think about this. The dates for low, mid, and peak seasons for many hotels are set in stone. If May 15–August 15 is high season, why not plan your vacation for the week before or after? You'll still get that warm summer sun, but without the high season rate.

Another good example is the Smoky Mountains region. January and February are great months to view the wildlife along Cades Cove and to hit the outlet centers of Sevierville and Pigeon Forge, Tennessee. Bargains are everywhere, including conveniently-located, quality accommodations as low as $20 a night.

Call the right number. Whenever possible, call accommodations direct. An individual hotel may be offering a special package or rate that's considerably cheaper than the standard rate for their chain; using those nationwide toll-free numbers may cause you to miss out. Most accommodations have their own direct toll-free numbers, but even if it means a toll call rather than a toll-free, contact the specific hotel where you're wanting to stay.

Ask. Do you offer a seniors discount? Travel club? Student? What about a corporate rate? Did I say a corporate discount? Back in my days as a hospital employee, I phoned a hotel to make a reservation for a weekend getaway for my sweetie and me. Granted, this was a really nice place, but the price was still much higher than I'd expected.

As I rattled off every possible discount I could think of, the reservationist interjected, "Do you qualify for corporate?"

"Well, I do work for UAB hospital," I told her, "but this trip is for me and my husband—it really isn't business-related."

"That's not a problem," she explained. "I simply have to indicate that you are a corporate employee." That said, the rate dropped by more than a third.

If you have any hope of qualifying for some type of discount, ask. Remember, these folks want to rent you a room. If at all possible, they'll come up with a discount.

Book online. Many hotels have their own websites and offer internet specials and discounts. Use a search engine to locate the sites that you're interested in and see if online booking can save you some money. Remember, once you've checked out the site, you can still phone the hotel for more information before making a decision.

If you do choose to book online, make sure you key in any eligible discounts.

Coupons. Rest stops, service stations, and restaurants often maintain racks of discount accommodations booklets such as the Exit Information Guide. These booklets are area-specific, in that if you pick one up in Missouri, it will feature discounts for accommodations throughout Missouri.

These coupons can definitely save you money, but be

aware of the fine print, such as holiday and special event exemptions, weekday limitations, expiration dates, and more. Too, most require you to present the coupon in person, so advance reservations won't guarantee you the rate on the coupon. (Printable coupons are also available online at www.roomsavers.com.)

Make your list. Here we go again! Grab those pads and pencils and jot down everything that interests you in the way of a place to stay, then number them according to their importance. This will be a great help when you start calling places to check rates and availability.

There are many types of accommodation out there: motels, hotels, B&Bs (bed and breakfast), inns, condos, campgrounds, RV rentals, and more. Not all of these will apply in every situation, but here are some things to ask:

1. Are you offering any specials on [*whatever dates you have in mind*]?

2. What are your low/ mid/ peak seasons?

3. Are non-smoking rooms available?

4. Are refrigerators and/or microwaves in the rooms? (A number of places even offer extended stay facilities with sitting areas and kitchens.)

5. Is there a bathtub, shower, a combination, or both?

6. Are the beds queens or doubles? (If you're sleeping two folks to a bed, this could be a fairly important factor.) Is a room with a king bed available? If so, is there a difference in the room rate?

7. Do you have inside and/or outside corridors? (I don't know about you, but especially whenever I'm traveling on my own, I prefer my room to be inside a building rather than along an open walkway.)

8. Do you have elevators? If not, are ground-level rooms available? (This isn't a "duh" thing. I've stayed as high up as the third floor with no elevator on the premises —no fun at all when it comes to hoisting luggage.)

9. Is there an additional charge for parking? (Parking fees are becoming much more common and can easily run $8–$15 a day or more.) Is valet parking an option? Is the parking area a deck, open lot, what? Is it well-lit? Is there security?

10. Is breakfast included? If yes, what does it consist of? One chain's "continental" breakfast consists of a bag of warm orange juice and cold muffin hung on your doorknob, while others include a full breakfast buffet.

11. Do you have a pool? Indoor or out? Is it heated?

12. What about an exercise area?

13. A spa?

14. What about pets? Since furry family members are now frequently included on vacation, more places are beginning to welcome them. Those that do often have restrictions as to the pet's size. One pet-friendly place I've been is the Freeport Inn in Freeport, Maine. (A guide for accommodations that accept pets is located online at www.petswelcome.com.)

Let's say Hotel A has a heated pool, elevators, and indoor corridors for $65 per night.

For the same price, Hotel B offers a heated pool, elevators, and indoor corridors. Which do you choose? Hopefully you'll ask for more information, because Hotel A includes a free breakfast, while Hotel B does not, and Hotel B charges a $12 per day parking fee. Asking the right questions can save you big-time.

Have You Any Room?

Wherever we travel, we need a place to rest our weary heads, don't we? We need to know that we'll have a place to spend the night. We need a room.

But as we think about rooms, I want you to focus for a minute on a room that's a lot nearer and dearer, a room that's a whole lot closer to home. And that is the room in your heart.

The apostle Paul writes in Romans 10:8–9: "The word is near you, in your mouth and in your heart . . . if you confess with your mouth Jesus as Lord, and believe in your heart . . . you will be saved." Twice in that passage we read the words "in your heart." Here is where there must be room for Jesus. Here is where His Holy Spirit indwells the ones who have trusted Him with their lives.

Vacations are great, but eventually you have to come home. While that room away from home is fun for a time, you sooner or later feel the urge to head back, don't you?

Can I ask you something? Has there ever been a time in your life when you made room in your heart for the Lord Jesus Christ? If you have, I'm so thankful. But what about now? Is your commitment to the Lord Jesus Christ your first priority? If not, your life's out of order.

Maybe you've wandered from your first love. Won't you come home today? Your journey can have a happy ending. It's already been written, as a matter of fact: "his father saw him and felt compassion for him, and ran and embraced him and kissed him" (Luke 15:20). Your Father wants you to come home. Please don't delay.

If you haven't accepted Christ as Savior, what better time could you choose than this very minute? The book of Hebrews repeats these words three times: "Today if you hear His voice, do not harden your hearts" (Hebrews 3:7, 3:15, and 4:7). Each time the Holy Spirit calls to you and you ignore Him, you also reject Him—and rejecting the Holy Spirit hardens your heart, making it more and more difficult for your spiritual ears to hear His voice.

There is no room as important as the one in your heart. Make certain that the Lord of Hosts dwells within it.

For those who are children of the Living God, let me ask you: Do you take the Lord along on vacation? Of course you do. For, as God declared to the writer of Hebrews, "I will never desert you, nor will I ever forsake you" (Hebrews 13:5).

Do you consciously include Him? Does your quiet

time go along with you? Is worship with a corporate body of believers included? (Believe it or not, God has other sheep besides those in your own little flock!) God doesn't take a vacation from you! Please don't take one from Him, either.

While you secure your next room, think about the One who occupies your heart's room. And as you pack for that next trip, make sure you've made room for your very best Friend.

Airfare

Airfares are astounding. Two people on the same plane sitting in the same section of the aircraft might have paid fares that differ by hundreds of dollars! Why? Knowing the ropes about booking airfare can make all the difference in the world.

Booking Online

The best buys are online, folks, so for those of you who have yet to join the cyberspace community, airfares alone are a good reason to get on board. Virtually every airline posts weekly specials and sends them via e-mail directly to the people on their subscriber lists. Subscribing is free, and you can always delete the unopened messages whenever you're not shopping for airfare.

Where do I sign up? Each airline's website includes step-by-step instructions on registering to receive their Internet specials. Even if you don't want to sign up, most offer discounts for using their online reservation service.

Other businesses such as www.farebeaters.com and www.bestfare.com can also save you big-time on airfare.

How do I know if it's a good deal? The best way I can answer that is with an example. When booking Southwest Airlines (www.iflyswa.com) reservations online, you are directed to a screen that shows you the available fares for the flight you've selected. Even though you're looking at a particular flight's information, there are a surprising number of fares from which to choose.

Naturally, going over to the far, far right (the deepest, darkest corner) shows you the very best fare. The screen will also indicate which fares have already sold out and which ones are still available. Booking online will require the use of a credit or debit card, so have that handy. (Remember: if using a credit card, go ahead and mail the ticket amount to your credit card company—they always welcome advance payments.)

Ye Olde Telephone

You can still make your airline inquiries by phone, too. When you call, make sure you have your credit or debit card ready. If you want to avoid using either, you can tell the reservationist that you'll be picking up your tickets at the airport, but you'll need to take care of this within 24 hours. Otherwise your reservation will automatically be cancelled.

Ticketless Travel?

Today's travelers need not worry about paper tickets, either. While in most cases you can insist on having a real live paper ticket sent to you (or picked up at the airport), "ticketless travel" affords you one less thing to keep up with.

Your confirmation number (usually a series of letters and numbers) is all you need. At the airport on the day of your flight, simply present that information and proper identification at the appropriate airline ticket counter and you'll be on your way.

Sit!

In an orderly fashion. Airlines like Southwest offer open seating, which means they don't assign seat numbers. As passengers check in at the appropriate gate they are given numbered boarding cards. Numbers 1–30 have the first opportunity to board and select seats; 31–60 are next; and so on.

Ahead of all of these, though, are the "pre-boards." All airlines allow people with small children and those with difficulty walking (or other disabilities that might interfere with normal boarding procedure) to board the plane first.

Other airlines assign seating, which means that you

can request a specific seat or at least a window or aisle seat at the time you make your reservation. Seats in the emergency exit areas generally offer a bit more legroom, so some people like to request these seats. The only stipulation for acquiring a seat on this row is that you must be physically able to assist in an emergency (as in opening the emergency exit).

Bulkhead seats also have extra legroom (the first row of seats in a section) that can really add to your comfort on a long flight. Aside from the first class area (which offers roomier seats and more leg space), these spots are as good as it gets. They're usually taken early, but it doesn't hurt to ask.

Standby!

You've probably heard of someone who had to fly "standby," meaning that the person has a ticket for a different flight, but waits at the gate in case a seat comes available for an earlier flight. Once the final boarding call has been made, passengers flying standby are allowed to fill empty seats. Flying standby ain't always a bad thing.

Whenever I'm not in a big hurry to get from Point A to Point B, I'll check the departure screen (a monitor listing the outgoing flights and times) to see the time for the next flight for the airline I'm ticketed with to the destination I'm ticketed to. If it's not too long a wait, I'll go to the counter and volunteer as a standby passenger.

What did I just do? I told them that if the flight I was to be on was overfull (this does happen), I was willing to wait for the next available flight to my destination. Why would I be so nice? Because the usual reward is a free (good for up to one year) roundtrip ticket (generally limited to within the continental U.S.) or at least a substantial amount ($200 to $400) in airline credit vouchers.

Bear in mind before you decide to try this that *there is no guarantee that there'll be room for you on the next flight*.

I've also experienced this as a non-volunteer. On one occasion I was in a small airport awaiting a commuter flight when I heard my name being called over the speaker system. Arriving at the counter I was told that the plane was too full and that my name had been randomly selected to be pulled off that flight.

Had I protested that I had a pressing schedule or other situation, I'm sure they would have opted for another passenger, but I really didn't mind. For my trouble I received a free 10-minute phone card (so I could call ahead and relay my flight change to those awaiting me), a meal voucher (good for up to $8 in the airport's food court), and $400 in airline credit vouchers.

A Family Crisis

Airline workers are people, too, and they are often very understanding when a family emergency arises. If you need a flight because of a death or serious illness among your relatives, tell the ticket agent as soon as you phone or walk up to the counter. ***They cannot assist with a crisis they are not aware of.***

Yes, you'll be required to offer some proof of your situation (a patient name and hospital, funeral home information) but the airline will do its very best to get you to your needed destination as quickly and as inexpensively as possible.

Auto Rentals

Reserve, reserve, cancel. Yep, the same system that works for accommodations will work for auto rentals. Once you've found a good rate, book it. If you find a better one, book it, too. Just be sure to go back and cancel the first one—and don't forget to keep a record of all your reservation and cancellation numbers.

Best buys. Again, there are great specials available via the Internet. Sites like www.expedia.com and www.travelnow.com are among hundreds that comparison shop for you and then show you the prices and companies they've found.

Personally, I don't mind checking each rental agency's site myself—and I often find a better buy for my effort. Too, rental car agencies all post specials, so if you're interested, you can sign up on their sites and begin receiving notices via e-mail.

It's in the mail. Credit card statements and junk mail often include coupons for free upgrades, discounts, and free rental days. (Of course, unless you're paying your balance in full each month, I hope you're not receiving any credit card statements!) If you're planning to rent a car, ask your friends and family to be on the lookout for these.

Don't Pay for What You Don't Need

First, let me ask you: Do you have full coverage insurance on your personal auto? If you answered yes, then as long as you're traveling within the U. S. of A., your insurance should also cover the vehicle you've rented. Check with your agent to be sure. Would a man with 20/20 vision pay for glasses? I would hope not. And neither should you pay for anything that isn't necessary.

Mileage. Far too many rentals are available with unlimited mileage for you to ever run the risk of having to pay for extra mileage. Make sure when you rent that your agreement does not specify a limited amount of mileage.

Can't fuel me. At the rental counter you'll be offered the choice of refueling the car yourself or prepaying for a refill and letting the rental folks take care of it when you bring back the car. Not only will the company's price for fuel be higher than what you could refuel it for yourself, but the charge will be for a full tank, regardless of how much fuel remains in the car when it's returned. I'd call this one a no-brainer for sure. Opt to refuel that vehicle yourself.

Just what you ordered. Most of the time the vehicle type you requested will be ready and waiting. On rare occasions, it won't. Sometimes a vehicle isn't returned on time or for some other reason is not available as expected. What do you do?

You insist on a discount if you're offered a lower category automobile. If you're offered a higher category, don't pay extra. Insist on the agreed-upon rental price—it's not your fault the car they promised you isn't there.

This is also a good spot to include this piece of advice: *Have a rental agent examine the car with you before you leave the premises.* Don't get blamed for scratches, dents, or other pre-existing damage on a vehicle. Make sure any blemish is on record with the agent before you take possession of the car.

Cruises and Combos

But It's So Expensive! Think cruises are too expensive for you? Hold it right there, missy! Let's do a little math. You're staying in a beachfront hotel and eating out for a week. Let's see.

The hotel is $150 a night, but you're getting your 7th night free, so that's only $900. Your breakfasts are included, so there's no expense there. Lunch is a fairly light meal for the two of you, so you only spend a total of $98 on that.

Dinner, a bit more pricey, comes to $210 for the week.

But what about little Biffy and Buffy, the kids? The hotel isn't charging extra for them and they're getting breakfast free, too. But their lunches and dinners have tacked on another $126. And those trips to play carpet golf and go to the water park and arcade cost $250 more.

So you've spent $1,584. Doesn't really sound all that bad if you never run the total, does it? Seems to me that's how we get ourselves into trouble in the first place. Hmmmmm. I seem to remember Jesus saying something like "first sit down and calculate the cost" (Luke 14:28).

Now let's look at a cruise. A 7-day Caribbean cruise costs $600 per person. But kids under 6 staying in the same room with their parents are free. The cost for the cruise? $1,200.

What's included? Virtually everything, food and all, with the exception of gratuities and some beverages. Onboard there are children's and adults' activities (you can participate or ignore), swimming pools, family-oriented live floor shows, a movie theater, onshore excursions, and more.

Sure, there are always some options that cost extra (skeet shooting comes to mind), but why? There are so many activities included in the cost, you'll never make use of them all!

Book 'Em, Danno!

With cruises, you either want to be the early bird or the latecomer. Booking early gets you the first choice on lower-priced cabins. The cheapest way to go is to opt for a lower level inside cabin. All you're going to do is sleep there, right?

Another perk about booking early is that if the cruise line oversells your type of accommodation, you'll be bumped up to a more expensive cabin at no additional charge. How early is early? Most cruise lines will welcome your booking a full year in advance of the sailing.

Those who book late can take advantage of leftover cabins and great reductions in normal fares. Reductions of 50% and more are not unusual.

How do I find these specials? The Internet is a great source, and so is the Sunday newspaper. Drop by your local library and flip through some current magazines' travel sections.

'Tis the season. Cruises also have high, mid, and low seasons, depending on the particular location. Low season specials can sometimes be spectacular—on occasion I've seen offers where 4 people can cruise for the price of 1 (all staying in the same cabin).

Getting There

Generally the fine print on a cruise ad will tell you airfare is not included. Add-ons for airfare to the departure port (usually, a shuttle will transport you from the airport to the dock) can be expensive, so it may be to your advantage to shop around and make your airline reservations independently. Whatever you decide, it never hurts to check.

Another option is to drive to the departure port. If the distance isn't too great or you've got the time to make the drive, you may save money even if you have to stop en route and spend the night. Make sure you *calculate the cost* for parking fees and ask about security.

Don't forget that there are other travel options such as Amtrak and Greyhound. Both advertise some impressive bargains now and then. (See www.greyhound.com and www.amtrak.com.)

Combos

Besides the air/cruise packages offered by cruise lines, some companies offer other combination packages that include airfare plus a resort stay. Watch newspapers, read magazine travel sections, and search online (for instance, try www.suncountry.com) for these types of packages. Last-minute and off-season rates for some of these combos can be incredible. Some resorts are all-inclusive, with accommodations and meals included at dirt-cheap prices.

The Travel Agent Is Your Friend

Did you know that many travel agents don't charge a fee? It's true. These folks or their companies profit in various ways, often by securing blocks of rooms or seats at low cost. This, in turn, allows them to pass the savings on to you.

Travel agents are professionals. If you belong to AAA or a similar organization, these services are a part of your membership perks. Check them out—you might be missing out on some fantastic bargains.

Even if an agency charges a fee, their ability to locate and book best buys may still be well worth these charges. Don't knock it till you've tried it—travel agents have found me rooms when I was sure there were no rooms to be found.

In the Driver's Seat

While your mind is on travel, let me ask you about your final destination. Can you say with absolute certainty that place will be heaven? One and all are invited: "Believe in the Lord Jesus, and you will be saved" (Acts 16:31). Have you ever trusted Jesus Christ to be the Savior and Lord of your life? If you have, your final destination is secure in Him.

As a believer in Jesus Christ, your final destination is heaven. Jesus Himself explained: "I go to prepare a place for you. . . . I will come again and receive you to Myself" (John 14:2–3). Whether through physical death or Christ's return for His bride, we will be forever in the presence of the Almighty Father.

Vacations are great, but I look forward to one trip that's gonna be clear out of this world!

Chapter 10

The Affordable Auto

"A chariot was imported from Egypt for 600 shekels of silver, and a horse for 150."

—1 Kings 10:29

"Something between a large bathing machine and a very small second class carriage."

—W. S. Gilbert, *Iolanthe*

Rent Before You Leap

If you're in the market for a new or nearly new car, why not rent before you buy? Instead of paying out gazillions of dollars for a vehicle that you've barely driven around the block, spend a little and save a lot—a lot of headaches when the car doesn't turn out to be what you expected.

Count the Cost

New versus used. Sure, that new car smell is exhilarating, but for $3, you can buy that fragrance in the car care section of your local discount store! The new won't last. Unless the interest rates are irresistibly low and you're able to negotiate the car deal of the century, it's better to let someone else pay that new car price—and own it long enough to work the bugs out. A low mileage, nearly-new car can save you thousands.

Insurance. Payments shouldn't be your only concern when auto shopping. How much is insurance for the vehicle you have in mind? Recently I compared two similar vehicles and found that one insured for 1/3 the cost of the other. Why? Fewer thefts, better safety records.

Is leasing an option for you? Maybe, maybe not. While you can get in with lower payments and less up-front money, the penalties for mileage above the agreed-upon limits can be astronomical. Also, whether you're happy with the vehicle or not, if your job situation or a medical emergency interferes with your ability to make the payments, you're locked into the timeframe specified in your agreement.

What's it worth? Books like the NADA (National Automobile Dealers Association) Blue Book are available at your bank, credit union, and local library. These list used car prices and give varying values according to mileage, overall condition, accessories, and other factors.

If you're considering a used car, know the approximate book value. And even if you're looking at a new car, unless you're planning a lifetime commitment, you'll want an idea of how well it will hold its value.

But it's so cute. Cute is nice, but you should want more in a car. What's the maintenance record for those babies? Grab a copy of *Consumer Reports* auto issue (at your local library) and see what these folks have to tell you. *CR* does independent testing on vehicles, so their info is unbiased.

Read more than the basic info. Oftentimes one model of the same vehicle is problem-prone while another may be very low maintenance. Let's say you're looking at a Felix. (Yes, I made that up.) While Felix Sport owners are reporting a minimum of complaints, Felix Deluxe owners have been plagued with problems. Sometimes the exact model you select can make a whole lot of difference.

Naturally, there are loads of websites where you can research and even shop for your used or new vehicle. While I don't want to recommend any particular site, be aware that there are plenty out there to assist you.

What are my options? Do you want room or mileage? Comfort or performance? Functionality or sleekness? Would you rather have a sunroof or a CD player? Every option that adds value adds cost, and every option also means more to maintain. While a convertible may look tempting in July, it might not be so enjoyable come winter.

Contrary to what advertisers and salesmen say, we really can't have it all. We have to make choices. Based on your average annual mileage, if one car's fuel economy means you'll put $2,000 in the tank and another means you'll only spend $700, which do you choose? It all depends on your needs.

Aren't wants to be considered, too? Absolutely. But first be certain your needs are met before you bring even the first want into the picture.

Make another list. Keep those pencils sharpened. Write down the things you really need in a car, whatever they are: room for four, all wheel drive, four doors, plenty of legroom, high MPG. Once all that's down, make the second list of wants: red exterior, gray interior, CD player and changer, sunroof, power locks, etc. Number these wants by priority.

Take both lists along when you start car-shopping. Don't let the cute red two-seater cause you to forget you need room for four passengers. Don't let a good-looking sunroof lure you into a car that has a history of leaks. Make sure what you buy will first meet your needs before even beginning to look at the aspect of wants.

Dealing with the dealer. If you do business with a dealer, you're going to pay more money. If you buy from an individual, your best bet is to make sure the car you're looking at has a fully transferable warranty—and be certain to inquire as to the cost of the transfer.

Other Stuff

"And there are also many other things."

—John 21:25

*"Indeed all the business of life, is to endeavour
to find out what you don't know by what you do;
that's what I called 'guessing what was at the other
side of the hill.'"*

—Duke of Wellington, quoted in *The Croker Papers*

Personal Pampering

Kick the soap. Is dry skin a problem for you? Stop using soap. Bar soap, that is. The ingredients that make bar soap stick together (to form a cake or bar) may be what's drying your skin. Switch to liquid bath products. Such as? Moisturizing shampoo. Why pay $12 and more for bath fragrances that do no more than the average moisturizing shampoo? Skin is protein, right? And so is hair. What's good for one is also good for the other.

Products like Suave, White Rain, and other bargain brands come in some great scents such as coconut, freesia, and more. All of these work beautifully as body washes. And liquids, unlike bar soap, leave no bathtub ring.

Get a leg up. Scraping soap into your pores as you shave your legs is another thing that helps make skin dry and itchy. Quit soaping before shaving—or spending on costly shaving cream products. Try hair moisturizer. It's smooth, fragrant, and guess what else? Moisturizing.

Love those gloves. Round up: (A) a pair of light-weight cotton gloves; (B) a pair of latex ones; (C) a pair of thicker all-cotton work gloves or two old socks; and (D) a bottle of hand and body lotion. You're about to be pampered.

Slather your hands with as much lotion as you can pack on. Slip your hands inside the thin cotton gloves. Top these with the latex ones, then pull the heavier gloves or socks over these.

Now start cleaning house. I know this wasn't what you had in mind, but who has time to sit around? As you clean (remember, you're waterproofed to clean anything), you're getting a salon-style hand treatment.

Can't you imagine how this is going to change things? I can just hear it: "That Millicent must clean house every day—her hands always look terrific." Try it. You'll almost look forward to cleaning.

Never admit de feet. Instead of complaining about those cracked, yucky heels and cardboard foot soles, do something about them—sleep in socks. At least once a week, slather on a rich lotion and sleep in a pair of thin cotton socks. At bath time, lightly rub rough heels with a steel wool soap pad. Be sure to apply a good moisturizing lotion once you have finished.

Oui, oui—it's free. How about a no-cost French manicure? You'll have to invest in the initial products, but you have some or most of these things already on hand. All you need is: (A) fast-drying nail polish in clear and white; (B) 1-inch wide masking tape; and (C) scissors.

Start with clean, shaped nails. First, cut the masking tape into narrow strips (about 1/8") and attach one edge to a lap desk or other surface where these can be readily removed. Next, apply one light coat of clear polish to each of your nails. Wait about five minutes, then apply the tape strips—one to each nail just where you want the white polish to begin. Make sure the tape seals securely in place all the way across each nail.

Now, take the white polish and lightly coat the area above the tape. Wait five minutes and do it a second time. Wait five more minutes, remove the tape strips, and apply a final coat of clear polish over the entirety of every nail.

Whenever I watch TV or talk on the phone (or both!), I make the time count double by doing my nails, too.

Swap Days

A fun and free way to collect up some new (or new-to-you) goodies and to get rid of the items you're ready to part with is to declare a Swap Day. When I was part of a Tuesday morning Bible study, we would declare an occasional Swap Day. Each person would bring any and all unwanted items and we'd dive in and go through each other's offerings.

We weren't all the same age and we weren't all the same size, but we always managed to find something we wanted that another one of us was giving away. I acquired new jewelry, purses, "what-nots," and more—everyone ended up with new treasures. Plus we got rid of our surplus, and no one spent a dime in the process!

Out and About

Soap saga. You dig around in the garden, finish up, and head for the garden hose. You reach for the liquid soap, but someone's left the top open and the contents have dripped out. You put out a bar of soap and, on your next gardening day, find it mired in grass clippings beside the faucet.

The solution is easy. Use a stray knee-hi or the leg of an old pair of pantyhose to safely keep that soap right where you want it. Drop the bar in the toe of the hose and tie the other end around your outdoor faucet. The soap will be there when you need it.

Grill warfare. Love foods that are cooked outdoors but hate the mess they make on your grill? Next time, before you light the grill, spray it with non-stick cooking spray.

Flower power. Whether you cut your own flowers from your garden or go out and buy them, stick them in the fridge each night when you go to bed. If vase and all won't fit, remove the flowers from the vase, wrap the ends in paper towels, and gently lay them on a fridge shelf or in a bin—be careful to give them plenty of space. These trips to the cooler will keep your flowers looking perky for several extra days.

Closing Comments

My friend Lisa Bledsoe stays in touch with me mostly through her prayers and e-mails. Many times I have felt the power of her prayers and appreciated her words of wisdom. I want to leave you with her advice about money: "Have cash for emergencies. You can always wait to buy a new television set, but if the transmission on your only car goes out, waiting and saving may not be possible."

Staying out of debt is important, but so is setting aside money for that rainy day. Even if you're still working to pay off a debt load, go ahead and start a savings plan now. Set aside $5 a week if that's all you can manage. But start immediately to discipline yourself and make preparation for your future.

Proverbs' virtuous woman "smiles at the future" (Proverbs 31:25). Why? Because: (A) she has entrusted her days to her Lord, and (B) she has been diligent to make preparation for whatever days may be ahead.

But there's also a C. This woman has also entrusted her eternity to God. Second Timothy 4:8 puts it this way: "there is laid up for me the crown of righteousness, which the Lord . . . will award to me on that day; and not only to me, but also to all who have loved His appearing."

Meaning what? The future of those of us who have placed our faith in the saving grace of the Lord Jesus Christ, who have believed on Him as the one true Lord and Savior, is secure. Yes, our earthly lives may have their ups and downs, but when we fix our eyes on Jesus (Hebrews 12:2), we can weather every storm and, like our Proverbs woman, smile at the future.

For more Bargainomics® info, visit
www.bargainomics.com